Bath

Bath

John Payne

INNERCITIES
Signal Books

First published in 2012 by
Signal Books Limited
36 Minster Road
Oxford OX4 1LY
www.signalbooks.co.uk

A catalogue record for this book is available from the British Library

ISBN 978-1-904955-93-1 Paper

Cover Design: Devdan Sen
Design & Production: Devdan Sen
Cover Images: Donal Hanna/istockphoto; Wikipedia Commons
Illustrations: Wikipedia Commons except p.86 John Payne; p.170 Simon
    Patrick; colour section: Wikipedia Commons except Bath in Time – Bath
    Central Library pp.5 (upper), 8-9, 10 (upper), 15 (both)
Maps: p.xi, p.184 courtesy Bath Tourism Plus (www.visitbath.co.uk)
Printed in India

Contents

Acknowledgements

The following individuals have been helpful in ways of which they may not even be aware: Nikki Bennett, Susan Boyle, John Bull, Gill Carter, Peter Clark, Barb Drummond, Rose Flint, Adrian Lewis, Anthony Mayer, Crysse Morrison, Sandra Payne, John Peverley, Steve Poole, Cathryn Spence and Hugh Torrens. For any errors in the book, I take full responsibility.

Special thanks to:

Adrian Arlib for his photos of the Whitecroft Woods roads protest which I have not used directly but which inspired me to think laterally about Bath; Malcolm Aylett of the Friends of Bath Jewish Burial Ground; Rashad Azami of Bath Islamic Society, Imam of the Al Muzaffar mosque; Father Richard Barton and Rupert Bevan at St Alphege's Roman Catholic Church in Oldfield Park; Joe Bennett, Bath Spa University; Emma Cross, Bath Mozart Fest; Bob Draper at Bath Royal Literary and Scientific Institution; Kirsten Elliott and Andrew Swift of Akeman Press; James Ferguson of Signal Books; Tim Graham of Millstream Books; Charlotte Hanna at Thermae Bath Spa; Lynne Hardy at The Genesis Trust; Bridget Johnston for reminding me of the debt Bath owes to Brian Greenhalgh; Colin Johnston and colleagues at Bath Record Office; Caroline Kay at the Bath Preservation Trust; Ruth Knagg, Bath Literature Festival; Sarah Lewis and Rosemary Emsley of the Widcombe Association; Simon and Elaine Rogers of Rickard's, Northumberland Place; Bishop Beth Torkington of the Moravian Church; various local history societies and websites in Bath for information and responses to my enquiries; officers of Bath and North East Somerset Council, especially Mark Williams, for information about the hot springs, and Jon Poole for help with population statistics; staff and volunteers at many museums in and around Bath, especially Stuart Burroughs at the Museum of Bath at Work, Stephen Clews at the Roman Baths Museum, Amy Frost at Beckford's Tower, and Katie Jenkins and Amina Wright at the Holburne Museum; staff and members of the Bath Ethnic Minorities Senior Citizens' Association (BEMSCA); staff at All Saints Church and Centre Weston, Julian House, and BANES Racial

Equality Council; staff at Bath Spa University library, Frome and Bath libraries (especially Anne Buchanan and Mary Henderson) and through them the all-too-often unacknowledged national inter-library loan system.

This book is dedicated to my sister Mary and my brother David,
and in memory of our parents
George Herbert Payne and Bessie Mary Yeo

Bath City Centre

Map Key

	Tourist Information	D5		Pedestrians only	
	Architectural Interest			No Access point	
●	Place of Interest		**P**	Car Park	
	Parks and Gardens		**P**ride	Park & Ride Bus Stop	
WC	Toilet		**D**	Disabled Parking Bay	
G	Cinema			For further information on parking	
†	Church			and Park & Ride services go to	
X	Sport and Leisure			www.bathnes.gov.uk	
	Hospital (no A&E)	C4		or call 01225 477133/4	
	NHS Walk in Centre	D5	**T**	Taxi	
✉	Post Office	D4	🚌	Bus Station	D6
	Shopmobility	D5	🚆	Railway Station	D6
	Library	D4		Coach Park	C5
				Police Station	E5

Widcombe Old Church

1 | Contours
Geography and Topography

"The grandeur of the setting, with the great curve of the river containing and defining the thickly wooded slope from which issue two rivulets of steaming water, would have been a familiar, if awesome, sight—somewhere, surely forbidden to ordinary men, where the gods dwelt. And for those bold enough to penetrate the tangled wood to its heart there would have been an even more remarkable scene—the bubbling waters gushing upwards through black quicksands fringed by matted vegetation and boulders, all bright red, stained by the oxidized iron salts in the water."

Barry Cunliffe, *The City of Bath* (1987)

The city is there, somewhere beneath us. Thick snow beneath our feet and a swirling misty frozen rain (or sleet, or snow) falling gently from grey skies stained with yellow. The city is not only contained but hidden far below us. For Bath, the setting is all. There may be architecturally more interesting cities, culturally more lively cities, cities where the conflicting interests of motorists and pedestrians, residents and visitors, locally born and incomers are fought over with greater passions, but for Bath the city begins with the setting, the balance of landscape and built environment. That air of a city that knows its place in some greater scheme of things.

Even on a deep winter's day like today. To the north-west of the city, the little clump of trees on Kelston Knoll floats unsteadily in the sky, a charcoal blur above a landscape only differentiated from the sky by the light grey of the snow-fields, and the dark grey stains of trees and houses. Lansdown is up there somewhere in the murk, that bold outrider of the Cotswolds where daring deeds were done during the English Civil War and William Beckford built his golden tower. And climbing up it are the crescents and terraces, from the stern classicism of the Royal Crescent and the strange symbols of the Circus to the less known, unfinished Camden Crescent and airy Lansdown Crescent. Off to the left, in Bath's shy south-eastern corner, the secrets of Prior Park and its landscaped gardens, Widcombe with its late medieval church, its pretty baroque manor and the locks of the Kennett and Avon Canal, Lyncombe with its motley assortment of Victorian villas, all quite different from the Georgian splendours flowing northwards from the city centre.

Immediately below us as we stand in the protection of the Sham Castle folly lies the city itself, carefully skirted by Brunel's Great Western Railway, the gothic abbey, the late, late Victorian extravagance of the Empire Hotel, the flaming twenty-first-century modernity of the new spa building with its rooftop swimming pool, the intimate shopping streets and passages, the Georgian elegance of Queen Square and North and South Parade. And somewhere deeper still lies the secret of the waters, the hot springs which have proved so alluring to successive people settling on the banks of the River Avon: British, Roman, Saxons, Normans. Bath, the great pleasure-ground of England, loved by some, disapproved of by others, in part a local place, a provincial city, but also recognized as of international importance, one of the few World Heritage Sites in the whole of England.

Above our heads in Rainbow Woods, carefully protected and managed by the National Trust, the trees gather protectively against both winter storms and summer sun. But not today a green shade, rather a black cobweb of branches and twigs, and beneath our feet the rustle of dead and frozen leaves peeping from between banks of snow. There is mystery in the woods, the faces of friends long scattered across the world, the sound of children playing, shouting, laughing, crying, the quiet voices of loved ones, the sense of the unrelenting onward march of the seasons and the years, the heavy silence of a snowbound landscape, of time stopped in its tracks, time frozen, time reversed.

City of Water

Of all the secrets of the city of Bath, the deepest and most mysterious is that of the waters. Every great city has its theory of origin, of why and when it came into existence. The prehistoric people in this part of the world were not much interested in the boggy river valley. Their lives centred on hilltop forts which could be defended in times of strife. The closest to the present city centre is Bathampton Down, up behind Sham Castle and the university, now rather incongruously stranded in the middle of Bath Golf Club. Across the valley to the north-east, dominating the ridge between the Swainswick and St. Catherine's valleys, lies Little Solsbury (or Solsbury Hill).

Yet it is quite wrong to think of this as a far-flung corner of barbarian Europe, awaiting the arrival of imperial Roman enlightenment. Traders from the Mediterranean, Greeks and Phoenicians, had long been aware of the metal deposits in the Mendip Hills and from time to time had come to these shores for trading purposes. There is evidence of a well developed culture here, with extensive farming settlements more appropriate to the arts of peace than the rigours of warfare. The current archaeological consensus is that rather than resisting the arrival of the Roman legions in 43 CE, the local British (Celtic) tribes were only too keen to welcome them and share the new technologies in building and agriculture of which they had already become aware because of their links with continental Europe.

The story of the leper king Bladud and his pigs, cured by the healing waters of the springs, is probably more myth than recorded history. But it is just one way of representing the simple fact that the curative properties of the springs were almost certainly known to the Celtic population of the area, long before the Romans turned Bath into their favourite pleasure resort, the one place in cold, wet Britain where warmth and comfort could always be guaranteed. Healing properties or not, just wallowing in hot water has to be one of life's constant pleasures, regardless of the time and culture we inhabit. The Romans—and here we might usefully contrast the approach of later empire-builders—were sensitive to local cultures. The sacred springs were thought to be the haunt of the Celtic god Sul, who could be easily annexed to Minerva, the Roman god of healing and wisdom. The life-size gilded bronze head of Sul Minerva, found in a sewer trench in Stall Street in 1727, may well be part of the original Roman cult statue presiding over their temple area. She remains one of the loveliest remnants of imperial Rome to survive in distant England, and is on display in the Roman Baths museum.

But the Romans did more than build a temple for their goddess. They built a large complex of ritual baths where citizens and pilgrims could immerse themselves in the hot, sulphurous waters. No longer was Sul Minerva to be allowed to skulk among the boggy undergrowth. The Roman name for Bath—Aquae Sulis, the waters of Sul Minerva—confirmed the linking of the older beliefs to Roman power and organization. Like all sacred springs, the place where the hot waters bubbled up to the surface was seen as a meeting point of the day-to-day world and the spirit world. The gods needed to be placated, most noticeably by the offering of coins. One particular feature of Bath that has come to light in recent excavations is the range of messages written to the goddess on metal plaques, often asking for vengeance on enemies. Gods and goddesses were serious business, not just a holiday sport.

In the post-Roman period, the temple precinct and the baths silted up, but it now seems that at no point was belief in the therapeutic value of the waters abandoned. During the Middle Ages several charitable hospitals clustered around the baths to provide accommodation for the poor. Bath continued to attract the sick and lame of all social classes, and whatever the contested nature of the actual healing value of the waters, they returned home satisfied, as much by the break from routine, the fun and games of Bath, the good company. Yet this emerging leisure industry was still only a side-issue for Bath. Although it is hard to imagine it today, Bath in 1700, before the great Georgian building boom, looked and lived much like other prosperous Cotswold wool-towns.

The hot springs are back in business once more. The Three Tenors—Josep Carreras, Plácido Domingo and Luciano Pavarotti—sang at a free, open-air concert in front of the Royal Crescent on a balmy summer evening in 2003 to celebrate this great event. As it happened, they were three years too early. Paint was peeling from the freshly-painted walls, snags were appearing between design and execution. The costs were escalating, and the local authority had become embroiled in an unseemly series of quarrels with the architect and contractor. But open they did as Thermae Bath Spa in 2006, and the general consensus is that the project has been a wild success. Splashing around in the hot, pungent waters of the rooftop pool on a crisp winter day, with the surrounding Bath stone buildings etched against a blue sky, will always be a powerful experience of the force, the generosity and the mystery of nature. And mystery it is. Still no-one knows where the waters come from. The most probable location lies in a deep aquifer somewhere below the Mendips. It is assumed that such a giant underground reservoir exists, but it has never been seen. Perhaps the waters represent the rainfall of a few hundred years ago; others with equally fine scientific credentials have proposed up to 10,000 years ago.

The elegant little Cross Bath, the most authentic relic of the Georgian baths complex, tells its own story of the great revival of Bath as a spa. By the twentieth century Bath was a more workaday, more ordinary city. Swimming, rather than bathing, was all the rage, and a public swimming pool at Beau Street was constructed in 1923, using the spa waters, suitably cooled. The Cross Bath declined in status to become the "Tuppenny Hot". It ended the twentieth century as a tumbledown if upper-class duck pond. Built directly above one of the three spring outlets, it is now the spiritual centre of the new complex, albeit ignored by the majority of visitors. The poet Ted Hughes described water as "the ultimate life—the divine influx", and these are the words carved around the rim of the water sculpture by William Pye through which the spring waters pass into the Cross Bath—the point at which the springs rise to the surface under natural artesian pressure. But what produces the pressure? There is a vast secret here, hidden forever from us in the geology of the Mendip hills. So to float in the Cross Bath is partly to be in tune with the spirit but also to be reminded how very little we know about the world we live in.

There is a lot of water in and around Bath which is nothing to do with the hot springs, although it was used of course by the Romans for their cold plunge pools and villas, which often included bathing complexes. Springs rise all round Bath, gurgling quietly between the Upper Oolitic limestone and Fullers earth strata (the upper streams) or between the Lower Oolitic and the clay (the lower streams). Sometimes they form small brooks, which join up and form more substantial streams to then become tributaries of the River Avon. Running down from the north side of the valley are the By (or Box) Brook, the streams of the St. Catherine's and Swainswick valleys and the Locksbrook. Just as the hot springs were regarded as sacred sites, so some of the other springs acquired a special significance. At Charlcombe Vale, tucked away as it were round the corner from much of Bath, up above Larkhall, something of this special significance of the springs can still be experienced. Charlcombe church, the oldest in Bath still in current use, has an exquisite circular Norman font in the form of a chalice. It is set up on a little knoll. In front of it and falling away to the lane is a garden, open to the public and cared for by the Quiet Garden Trust. And in the corner of the garden is the spring, the holy well of St. Mary's (also known as the Monks' Well). It was reputed to be good for the eyes, and is exceptionally pure. Local children are still brought there for Christian baptism in the open air.

Other springs and streams have been less successful in the modern world. The Locksbrook through Weston and Lower Weston is almost entirely culverted. Others disappear into modern drains. Brook Road in Oldfield Park suggests a stream course, but there is no sign of a brook (other than water pouring down the hill on a wet day). The Moorfields Brook just along the hillside has done rather better, helping to create a delightful watery play area below the Moorfields Estate, Bath's first (and best?) attempt at post-Second World War council housing. The medieval southern entrance to the city—Holloway—was once a stream and its waters were carried across the bridge into the city for use of the abbey. At Bathwick, the late Georgian and Regency eastwards extension of the city was across an area renowned for its springs. In return for the city fathers putting up money for the building of Pulteney Bridge, which links the Bathwick Estate into the city centre, they acquired rights over water from the Bathwick springs. Before there were streets here, there were pleasure grounds called Spring Gardens.

Springs and streams were not just important contributions to spiritual and physical health. They also supported local industry, stretching back to the Middle Ages. Brewing, cloth-making and tanning all flourished. The amount of dirty laundry produced by the playboys and girls of eighteenth-century Bath supported a major local industry, especially at Weston, which boasted not just the Locksbrook, but a dozen or more clear springs on the surrounding hillsides. It was deemed women's work, and the washerwomen of Weston gained a considerable reputation as strong, independent and hard-drinking. Jane Austen enjoyed the walk out to Weston, but does not make reference to its Amazonian residents who kept Bath in clean linen. Others found them a cause for scandal, particularly their reluctance to observe the Sabbath. Old habits die hard, and despite the Victorian temperance movement, Weston still had one pub per 216 residents in 1914, high even by Bath standards.

The River Avon

Springs hot and cold apart, the main water feature of Bath is the River Avon. Rising in North Wiltshire, it flows in a generally southerly direction across the fertile plains of the county, a landscape dotted with market and weaving towns and innumerable villages. But at Bradford-on-Avon it turns back north through the pretty wooded Limpley Stoke Valley before making its last definitive turn westwards towards the sea, beneath the heights of Bathampton Down and Little Solsbury.

The Avon has not always been kind to Bath. Until well into the twentieth century it was prone to flooding, and these unfortunate occurrences increased with frequency as the area to the west of the city became industrialized, with traditional water meadows built over and the river squeezed between stone walls. Unable to spread out naturally across the meadows, the river wreaked vengeance on the people of Bath by flooding their houses and factories. Yet even before the age of industry, Bath had regularly underestimated the Avon. At Green Park you can still see how the Georgian houses stand above the flood plain, as indeed they do at North and South Parade. But at Avon Street, right next to Green Park, there were constant problems with damp and flooding that reduced fine Georgian terraces to sordid Victorian slums. In the twentieth century the remaining slums were replaced by deck access flats, car and coach parks and the technical college (City of Bath College). For a century Avon Street was the home of poverty, vice and middle-class moral panics, all of which have a long history in Bath. Slums they may have been, but they did provide homes of a sort for people, however unhealthy. And some at least thrived.

The penultimate great flood of 1960 submerged large areas alongside the river with water creeping and swans gliding up Southgate Street towards the city centre. The Old Bridge was fatally damaged in this flood and replaced by the present Churchill Bridge a few yards to the west. This explains the lack of alignment between the new bridge and the road arches in Brunel's Great Western Railway viaduct. The other major result of this flood was the rebuilding of the weir in the city centre; the present horseshoe-shaped weir and sluice gates, the brainchild of engineer Brian Greenhalgh, replaced an earlier straight weir which features in many iconic views of Pulteney Bridge and its shops. But it was too late to prevent the last great flood—that of 1968.

Despite the apparent solution to Bath's flooding problem, worries persist. Sir James Dyson's plan to convert the old nineteenth-century Newark Works of Stothert & Pitt the crane-makers, empty for twenty years, into a school of engineering design, eventually foundered not on the conservationists' concern for Bath's industrial heritage, but the Environment Agency's concerns about flood prevention at a key riverside site. Given Bath's difficult relationship with its river, it is only at the Parade Gardens, which occupy the site of the old monastic grounds between the abbey and the river, that the river can be said to truly enhance the townscape. Here carefully laid out and manicured gardens provide pleasure and leisure for locals and tourists alike, together with the chance to enjoy Pulteney Bridge gleaming in the sunshine.

The river was at its most important during Bath's industrial period, from about the middle of the eighteenth century to the middle of the twentieth. The first step was to canalize the river between Bath and Bristol, second city of England and one of its most important ports. This involved putting in a number of weirs, as at Twerton and Saltford, though by restricting the river flow this arguably increased the risk of flooding. At about the same time Ralph Allen, who had made one fortune out of developing a network of postal services across England on the new turnpike roads, was about to make another fortune from the stone quarries at Combe Down. He constructed a tramway down past his showcase house of Prior Park along the route of what is now called Ralph Allen Drive. This meant stone could be easily transported to Bristol and onwards by sea to London, which Allen rightly identified as his chief market. At the next stage, the Kennett and Avon Canal was built from a junction with the river behind the present site of Bath Spa station, through Widcombe and the Limpley Stoke valley with its two splendid classical aqueducts, to eventually link up with the canalized River Kennet and provide a through route between London and Bristol. A narrow branch of the canal left the main route at Monkton Combe and penetrated into the heart of the North Somerset coalfield. This Somerset Coal Canal reduced the cost of coal for both domestic and industrial purposes in Bristol and Bath, and neatly bridged the gap until the coming of Brunel and the railway age.

The Great Western Railway brooked no rivals and by the middle of the nineteenth century had gobbled up both these canal companies. But whereas the Somerset Coal Canal was rapidly rebuilt as a railway line, the Kennett and Avon was left to moulder and decay at its own pace until in the 1950s a group of enthusiasts took it into their heads to restore it. This they did not just in sections, but the complete waterway, including the great rise of locks at Devizes which took the canal up from the Wiltshire plains into the Vale of Pewsey. It is one of the more encouraging stories of the twentieth century, of a group of men and women determined to prove the doubters wrong. Their reward is to see it now flourishing in an age of greater leisure and affluence, as a cycling and walking route, as well as providing for the barges old and new which chug along between the kingfishers, water lilies and reeds. A good case could be made that this is the best way of all to arrive in Bath, through the landscaped Sydney Gardens and then down the little flight of locks at Widcombe. But the days are long gone when the Broad Quay was the bustling heart of the city, with both agricultural and industrial goods being loaded and unloaded, creating wealth for the few and employment for the many.

Down here in the city centre, how conscious are modern Bathonians of the setting of their lives? It must be difficult not to have some sense of the city in its privileged landscape setting. The city fathers have allowed some growth, but especially from the middle of the last century onwards, and with the active support of the National Trust, they have acted decisively to defend the skyline that defines the city's limits. This sense of the built environment within the natural environment is most obvious from the Grand Parade, or from the open-air pool atop the new Spa building. Sham Castle is self-consciously present within this landscape, as are the Victorian villas lining Bathwick and Widcombe Hills up to the skyline of Claverton Down and Combe Down (a down is a flat hilltop and implies something altogether different from hill). The jewel in the crown of this landscape is Prior Park, built as much to be seen from the city, as for the fine views down across the landscaped gardens, lakes and Palladian bridge to the abbey and the rest of the city. Ralph Allen spent most of his time in a modest and comfortable town-house close to the abbey and the old Assembly Rooms. Prior Park was neither modest nor comfortable, and was built to advertise to the wider world the merits and potential of fine Bath stone—from Mr. Allen's quarries, of course.

North of the city centre, the great Georgian terraces and crescents climb the shoulder of Lansdown up to Camden Crescent and the lively Regency gem of Lansdown Crescent, which is rather further than most tourists get. The spire of St. Stephen's Church (nineteenth-century Gothic) dominates this particular view, with further up still the more discreet tower of the chapel at Kingswood School, a direct descendant of the school John Wesley set up for the boys of the tough mining community of Kingswood near Bristol. Later it became an important Methodist public school, and is now a co-educational school which still remembers its roots and its founder. But none of these developments reaches the Cotswold scarp of Lansdown itself, where William Beckford's beautifully restored golden-capped tower reigns supreme above the city he rather despised. The Admiralty, which arrived in Bath from London in the Second World War, well before renaming itself the Ministry of Defence, still occupies temporary single-storey accommodation up here. But like the sports fields, the race-course and the rather unlikely park-and-ride, the Admiralty huts do not intrude on the skyline.

To the south of the river, looking across for example from the Royal Victoria Park and the Royal Crescent, the view is less satisfactory. There was already some building here before the Second World War but the population, swollen by Admiralty families, was at bursting-point. The Germans had attempted to bomb the historic heart of Bath in the so-called Baedeker raids, targeting historic English cities such as Bath, Coventry and Exeter in retaliation against British bombing of historic Baltic port cities. At Exeter and Coventry they largely succeeded, but in Bath many of the bombs fell on the residential areas south and west of the city centre, thus aggravating the post-war housing shortage. The City Council response was to build the large council estates in Twerton, and also those around Odd Down, Southdown and Whiteway. Some of this new housing was very good indeed, some mediocre, but the overall effect was to intrude visually into the green setting of the city. Only the little cap of Twerton Round Hill, used as a park, introduces a softer note into this reach of the skyline, neatly matching the cap of the Cotswold outlier of Kelston Knoll, with its dark tuft of trees, across the river and a little further west.

If these twentieth-century additions to the city are intrusive looking south from the masterpiece of the Royal Crescent, this is not the case in the city centre, where Beechen Cliff rises so steeply and quickly from the river that it masks all the imperfections that lie behind. Jane Austen makes it clear in *Northanger Abbey* that, whatever her characters may think of the view, for her the author, this is "that noble hill, whose beautiful verdure and hanging coppice render it so striking an object from almost every opening in Bath." The very steepness of Beechen Cliff has saved most of it from development, but the demolition of the lower part of Holloway, Bath's steeply climbing historic route to the south, and its replacement by some very indifferent low terraced housing, was surely one of the greatest crimes committed against Bath during the late 1960s and early 1970s when no building outside the Georgian heartlands appeared safe from the City Council planners. Slum it may have been, but over 300 of the buildings demolished were pre-1875, including many worthy of restoration.

Of course, the view from Beechen Cliff, the setting of the city in its landscape, has changed. Once upon a time, compact, neat Bath within its medieval walls and gates, dominated by its monastic buildings, must have seemed quite overwhelmed by this grand setting. A Cotswold town, like others that have remained just that up to the present day, its stone gables of honey-coloured stone caught the golden rays of the evening sun in summer, and shrank back into modest grey on a chilly, overcast winter's day. Even in the nineteenth century, William Beckford, on his daily trips to Lansdown and the refuge of his tower, could look down on an uninterrupted view, across the Avon water-meadows and villages of Weston and Twerton to the Mendip Hills beyond. Nowadays the view is as spectacular but contains more prosaic elements: nineteenth-century villas, twentieth-century council housing on both sides of the river and the 1930s home of Bath City Football Club at Twerton Park. But curiously, there is no view of the set-pieces of Georgian Bath. Why this should be so is just one of the curious tales to be told in this book.

The Culture of Coal

It might have been very different...

Water is not all that lies beneath the surface of this smiling, green countryside. There is coal too. The Romans knew about the coal, though they were more interested in the lead and silver and gold they found higher up in the wild uplands of the Mendip Hills. It has been surmised that the perpetual flame in the temple precinct at Bath was coal-fired. From between 1750 to 1950 the coal industry flourished in the pit villages around Radstock. The closest mine to Bath was out at Newton St. Loe, only five miles from the city centre, a jewel of a Cotswold village on Duchy of Cornwall land. Extensive trials were carried out at Larkhall to the east of the city to determine the existence of coal but the bore-holes filled with water and were abandoned. Gainsborough noticed the coal-miners even during the Georgian period in a large landscape painting called "Peasants and Colliers Going to Market; Early Morning"—as Susan Sloman puts it, "the two major occupations of the rural poor in North Somerset".

Just twelve miles from Bath, but a world away, lies the mining town of Radstock. Coal-mining finished here in 1973, and it is now, quite literally, history. The most modern, most striking feature of Radstock town centre is the giant pit-wheel mounted on a rather fancy stone and metal column, which presides over the town's old market hall, now the Heritage Museum of the North Somerset Coal Industry (or Radstock Museum for short). The pit-wheel also looks down on the long abandoned tracks of two railways (Great Western and Somerset and Dorset) and the ugly bulge of the Radstock Co-operative Society, which continues to dominate retailing in the town. It offers food, clothing, domestic goods, furniture, travel and a funeral service. Behind the town, neat rows of stone-built miners' cottages climb the steep hillsides of the Wellow Brook valley.

Initially, coal was gathered at a few points where the coal seams were at the surface. In medieval times simple bell-pits allowed the extraction of shallow deposits. But not until the nineteenth century did steam power, winding gear and the canals and railways allow for the digging of deep mines and the distribution of coal to a wider area. The completion of the Somerset Coal Canal along the valley of the Cam brook led to a big reduction in the cost of coal in Bath, a benefit to householders and industrialists alike. Bath is built on coal, although it may wish to have as little to do with Radstock as possible. Furthermore, the smoke-blackened buildings familiar to those who grew up in Bath in the mid-twentieth century are a direct result of the use of coal for heating houses and powering factories. Areas such as Green Park, Norfolk Crescent and New King Street, adjacent to the engine sheds of the Somerset and Dorset railway and the marshalling yards from where coal was distributed to Bristol and beyond, were especially badly affected. But every building in Bath which used the honey-coloured Oolitic limestone was damaged to a lesser or greater extent.

As for social conditions, it is a moot point whether those in the North Somerset coalfield were worse off than those in Avon Street or the Dolemeads. Urban slums stemmed from a potent mixture of poverty, low pay, insanitary housing, overcrowding and ignorance. But conditions in a coalfield community could be more easily isolated and analysed. They were also more likely to become the subject of one of those moral panics beloved of Victorian England. Victorian prudery and prurience emerge too in the work of the 1840-42 Royal Commission on work in the mines. Much of the immediate public outcry centred on the moral outrage of scantily clad men, women and children working side-by-side underground. Yet in North Somerset, and indeed most of England, there is little evidence that women ever did underground work.

No-one wants to underestimate the appalling conditions in which men and boys worked in the mines, especially in Somerset where seams were narrow and faulted. In the Wellsway pit explosion of 1839, seven of the twelve miners who died were under twenty, including a boy of twelve and two aged thirteen. Eleven died at Newbury in 1859, seven at Timsbury in 1895 and sixteen at Norton Hill in 1908. Relief came in two ways, through the attitudes of pit owners and through collective action by mining families themselves. Some landowners such as the Duchy of Cornwall leased land for mining; among their tenants were the ambitious Mogg family, ancestors of the present MP for the area, Jacob Rees-Mogg. Others such as the beautiful and controversial Frances Countess of Waldegrave ran mines directly through a manager. She was responsible for sound workers' housing and public buildings in Radstock but could be ruthless during industrial disputes. Julie Dexter writes: "By contrast, Daisy, Countess of Warwick, whose husband owned much of the land to the northwest of the Somerset coalfield, was so taken with the plight of her husband's workforce that she introduced one of the first pit health schemes, installing a nurse at the Clutton Colliery before 1900, and was eventually ostracised by high society for her Socialist views." But essential reforms such as pithead baths had to wait until the twentieth century; those in Radstock date from the nationalization of coal-mining in 1948.

In the workplace, Somerset miners formed a union from 1872. It ran general campaigns for improved pay and conditions, but also supported local disputes such as that at Dunkerton in 1909. Nowadays Dunkerton is just another pretty village in the Cam valley, just two miles from the city boundary and the Odd Down park-and-ride. Then it was the largest pit in Somerset. Shots were fired during the 1909 riot—and not by the miners. The 1926 General Strike was especially bitter in Somerset. Mounted police were sent into the coal-field, while the Coleford miners marched to the nearby market town of Frome. Free soup was provided at the schools, and children were evacuated for several months to sympathetic families elsewhere in England.

Methodism made its own contribution to life in the coalfields, and it was always important in Bath, both as a criticism of the lavish, amoral lifestyle of the Georgian spa, but also in its direct concern for the poor and destitute, as we shall discover later in this book. But its foundations lay at Kingswood in the South Gloucestershire coal-field and in the North Somerset coalfield at Coleford, which Wesley called his "second Kingswood". For ambitious union men, the chapel gave experience of both public speaking and management.

Such then is the heritage of Radstock. But is it so very different from Bath? Class conflict, trade unionism, the co-operative move-ment, Methodism—all of these are part of Bath's heritage too. The dirt and noise of heavy industry are not something remote from the lives of older Bathonians, but rather the everyday experience of those who grew up there in the 1950s and 1960s. If the air today is purer, if the vast majority of Bath stone buildings are clean and well main-tained, if the cultural life of the World Heritage City takes people's lives beyond the humdrum and everyday, then that is fine and praise-worthy, and will be celebrated in this book. Equally, it will reflect some of the continuing inequalities and difficulties that Bath, in its own inimitable way, shares with the rest of twenty-first-century England.

The Roman Baths

2 | The Urban Map
Growth and Development

There are museums in Bath, but much of the city's history can be appreciated just walking around the streets. As a Unesco World Heritage Site, it is an old city that looks the part. For the less energetic visitor, there are the brightly coloured open-top tour buses with their loquacious guides—fine if you are sitting on the bus and it doesn't rain; less good in bad weather, and a positive menace when you are lining up the perfect photograph and a noisy, garishly coloured bus parks immediately in front of the view-finder. Yet Bath is not a picture book that can always be read and understood by the casual viewer. A case in point is offered by those "Georgian" buildings. They cover one hundred years from the 1720s into the Regency style of the 1820s, with the style modified according to the taste of the architect, or the purpose of the building. At various times in the Victorian period, more exercises in the classical style appeared in Bath. Then there are rather bland twentieth-century imitations and adaptations of the Georgian style. And finally the over-blown film-set architecture of the twenty-first century Southgate shopping centre

Roman Bath

What of the Romans themselves? How do they intrude into the cityscape? From York Street or the *piazza* to the south of Bath Abbey, the viewer is aware of what appear to be Roman statues rising above the parapet. The dress looks Roman, in a rather vague Hollywood way, but needless to say these are nineteenth-century decorations rising above the genuinely Roman Great Bath. Over the centuries the ground level in central Bath has risen. Thus all the Roman Baths and other remains of the Roman city are below ground level. When the Great Bath was excavated by archaeologists towards the end of the nineteenth century, it was opened up to the sky, with a superstructure of colonnades and statues above to advertise their work to the city. In Roman times, the Great Bath would have been roofed (first in timber, then with stone vaults). Artists' impressions of what this may have looked like are remarkably similar to a modern indoor swimming pool roof, and totally unlike the impression we have inherited from the Victorians. The open Great Bath is important for the visual links it makes between the various periods of Bath history—the Roman bathing pool, the abbey rising above it, the Pump Room and Ball Room that look down upon it, the nearby chimney of the Victorian laundry, a municipal enterprise that used the water from the hot springs—and the Bath skyline green and welcoming in the distance. As for those Victorian statues, this superstructure suggests vividly, in the heart of the city, a story: the story of Bath as an important Roman leisure establishment. To find out more involves another city, a lost city underground where the size and scope of the Roman leisure complex, with its hot and cold baths, its steam rooms, its banqueting suites, its sophisticated under-floor central heating, its temple, are still being uncovered. Roman Bath, like Roman Britain generally, is still work in hand.

This work in hand moves in two broad directions. Firstly the archaeological, although further progress here is hampered by the fact that little more can be uncovered without destruction of existing finds—there is a limit to how far back excavations can progress. We are looking, therefore, at a period when the great temple complex on the site of the hot springs was substantially complete in the early fourth century, by which time Roman Bath had been in existence for over two centuries. Secondly, there are changes in the way that archaeological finds are presented, with the static displays of objects found in the excavations, and of reconstructions of, for example, the great altar, complemented by audio visual displays and by some use of costume characters. Most visitors now use the individual audio guides which free them from the need to go round in a group, preventing bottle-necks as visitors pass through the complex.

The Hot Spring itself, from which the water emerges at 46°C, lies below the bay window, where visitors are tempted to sample the

Bath water as they pass through the Pump Room. Over the spring and the temple precinct was built the King's Bath which from medieval to Georgian times was the principal bathing-place. The goddess herself was treated not just as other worldly but as someone who might offer help and right wrongs in the world of the here and now. Offerings were thrown into the springs: twelve thousand coins have been found, while women often offered jewellery, combs or spindles. Messages engraved on sheets of pewter gave thanks for services rendered but also cursed enemies.

The rituals of bathing were those most familiar in modern "Turkish" baths, since it was in Byzantium that Roman rituals were preserved into modern times, with the sequence of hot bath, sweat rooms, massage and cold plunges. Because of the health-giving qualities of the waters, larger swimming baths are a feature of the facilities at Bath. The circular cold plunge is especially well preserved and by an odd quirk of history is now used as a wishing-well into which visitors can toss coins. In the early years of Roman Bath mixed nude bathing would have been the norm, but by the second century the Emperor Hadrian insisted on separate opening times for men and women. The existence of a later eastern range of baths suggests that eventually there were separate establishments for women and men. The mystery of the Bath waters is perhaps best experienced at the overflow drain, where the water disappears over a waterfall. Amid the steam, everything glows yellow, orange and red like a representation of the mouth of hell, the colours coming from the mineral deposits made over the centuries by the rich waters that have given life and purpose to this city

The Roman Baths have priority at all times in the use of the hot springs. This is the great money-spinner in the city, the unique attraction that brings visitors from all over the world. A surprising one-third of visitors to the Roman Baths come by coach, and for many overseas visitors it will be their only visit in England outside of London. The modern spa facilities (Thermae Bath Spa to give the official name) come second in the pecking order. In medieval times the outflow from the springs was used to power Isobel's Mill at Ham Gardens, part of the abbey lands between the city and the river. And then in Victorian times a municipal laundry used the waters, although by and large the mineral-rich waters have proved difficult to use in other ways. Thirty-five years ago Kit Pedler, environmentalist, television writer and the man behind the popular TV series *Doomwatch*, estimated that well over one hundred houses could be heated by the water flowing unused down the drain.

The Abbey

The Abbey Churchyard is the fulcrum of Bath, the point of orientation for an exploration of the heart of the city. On its south side lies the Roman Baths complex, with the graceful late eighteenth-century Pump Room and the later Concert Hall, which now serves as a rather grandiose reception room to the museum complex beneath. To the east lies the abbey church, the only remnant of a much larger monastic complex stretching eastwards towards the river. The west front of Bath Abbey is much loved, and much photographed, because it is both beautiful and available, so obvious to even the most casual eye. Bath was important in the early Middle Ages. It was border territory between Mercia and Wessex, and so an ideal place for Edgar to be crowned as first king of all England. The Normans preferred Bath to Wells, moved the bishopric here and built a large new Norman church. The subsequent quarrels between the canons of Wells and the monks of Bath were unseemly, lasted a long time and were not resolved until 1245 when Pope Innocent IV decreed that the bishopric would from then be known as Bath and Wells. It remains so. But it was Wells that gained the cathedral and Bishop's Palace, and the fame that comes from being the smallest cathedral city in England.

The West Front is one of the finest examples of that curiously English late gothic style; the Renaissance had arrived elsewhere in Europe, but England was being determinedly old-fashioned. It was only begun by Bishop Oliver King in 1502. King's dream of the angels descending and ascending between heaven and earth, which he claimed had inspired the project, is reproduced here in the Jacob's ladders placed either side of the soaring west window. There has been much restoration over the years, since any west front in this part of the world is vulnerable to the wet, west winds, and much debate on whether angels descend head first or feet first. But no-one seems to care over much. The grand west door with its complex surrounds is as fine a door as any in England, though it is only opened on special occasions. The business doors are smaller and rather discreet, fitted into the aisles of what is in essence a hall church.

At first, building progressed well. But the Reformation and the sale of monastic property put a halt to building work. The church, like other monastic buildings, was plundered for building materials—lead and stone—and the nave roof taken down. In 1572 what was left was donated to the people of Bath as a parish church. Queen Elizabeth visited in 1574 and left Bath Corporation in little doubt about her disgust at the state of the building. (The Corporation was the group of local traders and property owners who held legal responsibility for local government in the city, as explained in Chapter 4.) The church was completed, though the nave roof was a flattened, plastered vault, quite unlike the splendid fan-vaulting we see today, which was the work of the Victorian architect George Gilbert Scott, and matches the glorious vaulting of the choir. With the large collection of funereal monuments moved to the sides of the church, this creates a vista of light and airiness. There is no break from west to east, with the high altar pushed right up against the east wall, and the organ relegated to the north transept. The abbey serves Bath well, both as church and concert hall.

One final feature of the abbey that is very obvious from most vantage points in the city is the central tower. This is an oblong rather than a square, resting as it does on the foundations of one bay of the Norman nave. Its narrower side is best seen as part of the streetscape of the High Street, as described in Chapter 3, with the popular meeting place of the Rebecca Fountain immediately below it. Its broader side is best viewed from the rooftop pool of the Spa, where it dominates the view to the east, with the Bath skyline climbing away beyond. Touched by the setting sun, or illuminated after dark, it represents continuity in the city. While the tower of the abbey is in view, we can be quite sure that we are in Bath, the Queen of the West, as it has often been dubbed.

The Spa and Around

One indirect advantage of Nicholas Grimshaw's splendid new Spa building is the way it provides a clear context for the various charity hospitals that cluster around it, and which were previously rather obscured. The largest of these is the St. John's Hospital to the west, a fine set of buildings dating from various periods in the city's history. Established in 1190, it is one of the country's oldest active charities, and continues to build, most noticeably the new almshouses next door to the Lansdown Cricket Club in Combe Park. St. John's was built close to the Cross Bath to enable the poor to have easy access to the hot springs. The earliest surviving building is the chapel (1723), the first classical chapel built in the city, and still used for its original purpose. John Wood the Elder was very active here as a young man, but by the 1720s the hospital had fallen (temporarily) into the hands of the Duke of Chandos, who wanted to exploit the position of the buildings to provide lodgings for the fashionable visitors Bath was beginning to attract. In keeping with what was to later become standard practice in Bath, he used cut (ashlar) stone for the façade onto Chapel Court, whereas the façade that faces onto the Cross Bath and can be seen from the rooftop pool was in rougher rubble stonework more familiar in the small towns and villages of the Cotswolds and Mendips. At one time it was rendered to give a more polished finish, but this was removed during restoration in the 1990s.

On the Beau Street side of the Spa building is a large and rather messy nineteenth-century structure which for much of the twentieth century housed Bath Technical College. This was built as the United Hospital, the forerunner of the Royal United Hospital in Combe Park, now Bath's main hospital. It is empty at the time of writing, and may or may not become a five-star hotel. The other charity hospitals are Victorian as we see them today. Bellot's Hospital in Beau Street was founded in the early seventeenth century to accommodate poor visitors to the hot baths, and rebuilt in Victorian times, but the coat of arms (of Lord Burghley, for Thomas Bellot was his steward) above the door was saved from the original building. Round the corner in Bilbury Lane and again clearly visible to visitors to the Spa is St. Catherine's Hospital, built in Tudor style in 1829.

John Wood the Elder's work at St. John's Hospital was just the beginning for this young man. It was he who transformed the face of Bath in the first half of the eighteenth century. At first, the Georgians were content to put up new buildings spreading beyond the old city limits to the north-west. But conservation is a rather new fad in Bath, and later both Georgians and Victorians had no compunction at all in tearing down Cotswold houses of previous centuries and rebuilding the city in the classical or neo-Gothic styles.

In the beginning, then, was John Wood. But John Wood was very preoccupied by origins, and for him the origins were both magical and murky. There is little in Wood's early life to suggest the grandiose. Born in Bath in 1704, the son of a builder, he was apprenticed as a carpenter. After working in both London and Yorkshire, he settled back into his home city, not to enjoy its Cotswold charms but to transform it. He wanted to expand in two areas—north-west of the city, and south-east of the abbey. What we shall never know is whether there was ever a master plan, or whether Wood the speculative builder made it up as he went along. What he wrote fifteen years later in his *Essay towards a Description of Bath* (1742) gives no clear indication of what was in his head in the mid-1720s. Wood drew on two sources of inspiration, classical Rome and Ancient Britain, which he tried to fit together with each other. In his 1741 book *The Origin of Building* he has much to say about well-known Stonehenge and the much less well-known but equally interesting stone circles at Stanton Drew, a few miles south-west of Bath. All building, Wood thought, went back to the biblical Temple of Solomon, and this he believed was the source of both the work of Ancient Britain and Ancient Rome. God, according to Wood, had transmitted to Solomon a system of divine proportions, and the druids had used this in their stone circles. It is difficult indeed to reconcile Wood the speculative builder and Wood the speculative architectural historian.

Wood's first work, which set the tone for the rest of the century, was Queen Square, just beyond the old city walls to the north-west.

For this he used the Roman model that had come down via the Italian architect Andreas Palladio. It is simple, austere architecture which emphasizes the overall design of the terraces that make up the square rather than the individual houses. There is a clear break from the ornate, almost Baroque style of Widcombe Manor (earlier than Queen Square) and Rosewell House in Kingsmead Square which actually post-dates Queen Square. Michael Forsyth describes the latter as a "wild provincial Baroque that must have been as distasteful to Beau Nash as it was to Wood". (Wood was the architectural stylist of Georgian Bath, just as Richard "Beau" Nash, Master of Ceremonies, set the social tone for the city.)

If Wood the architect had a clear idea of how he wanted his square to look, Wood the speculator had more exacting tasks. Ideally the site would have been levelled, but that would have cost too much. The western side was built as three joined Palladian villas (which actually contained individual houses), but in the 1830s a rather heavy Greek Revival building was inserted; the eastern side is a row of disconnected houses stepped up the street. Yet Queen Square has survived well, despite being for much of the twentieth century part of the through A4 route to Bristol. The trees provide blossom in spring, shade in summer and colour in autumn, and generally disguise the less satisfactory features described above. Boules is played, there are occasional events such as food and art fairs and on a number of occasions at Christmas an ice-skating rink has been set up here

Circus and Crescent

Wood's masterpiece is, without doubt, the Circus. For the visitor who climbs steep Gay Street, past the Jane Austen Centre, it comes as a surprise. Suddenly the ground levels out and there is Wood's vision—British? Roman?—a fine circle of houses in three segments, observing the classical orders of Doric on the ground floor, Ionic and Corinthian above. For the eighteenth-century visitor, the impact would have been even more dramatic, because the plane trees, which now tower high above the houses, were not part of the plan. Wood was content with stone setts covering a central water reservoir. He lived to see the foundation stone laid in 1754 but not to oversee the buildings themselves. His son, John Wood the Younger, adhered to his father's plan, regardless of its idiosyncrasies. The acorns on the cornice are a clear allusion to the druids and also to one of Wood's heroes—the swineherd-king Bladud who is credited as the first to identify and use the healing properties of the hot springs. With the frieze above the Doric columns we enter a more complex world, that of freemasonry, the world of Mozart's *Magic Flute.* Kirsten Elliott, in her entertaining book on Wood, questions whether he was ever an active freemason, but clearly some of the symbols have masonic references. Others refer back to older emblem books, to alchemy, to the world of the Templars.

To his father's square and circle, Wood the Younger added the Crescent. Here I admit to prejudice. I do not like the Royal Crescent and never have done. I find the architecture heavy, overdone, especially those massive double height columns which link the first and second floors. Bladud has been supplanted by Rome as the preferred myth of origin of Bath. In my childhood the grassland in front of the Crescent was still in use as allotments, a wartime austerity measure. When the allotments were removed, we youngsters celebrated it as new place to play football and cricket rather than a place to admire eighteenth-century Georgian architecture. Later I discovered the untidy backs, the rear façades with their additions and irregularities which betray just how uncomfortable a place the Royal Crescent must have been to conduct anything like normal everyday life. And yet on a perfect summer's evening can I think of anywhere I would rather be, watching the evening sun light up the Bath stone until it glows pink and orange with delight? No, of course I cannot. It was much like that the evening of the Three Tenors concert, when Pavarotti, Domingo and Carreras sang for the people of Bath in weather so perfect that we seemed to have been transported for a few hours to another planet, another realm of reality. At some point in the history-of-architecture-free zone of childhood, something had been absorbed: that the Royal Crescent is about the relationship between nature (grass, trees, flowers) and building. In Georgian times this was part of the Bath Commons, now it is part of the Royal Victoria Park, for which we have the Victorian city fathers to thank.

Those who use the park may or may not be aware of the buildings; those in the buildings may or may not be aware of the open spaces outside. Yet there is a fit, and it is this fit—the countryside in the city and the city in countryside—which was to influence the later, higher crescents and terraces and the overall sense of why Bath matters, rather than the enclosed and very urban space of the Circus.

Not many tourists venture beyond the Circus and the Royal Crescent. Stout shoes, half-decent weather and not minding steep hills all help. Some hundred yards north of the Royal Crescent is St. James' Square, by John Palmer, with streets flowing out diagonally from each corner. The same architect may have designed Lansdown Crescent, the highest and perhaps the loveliest of Bath's crescents, and home to William Beckford. A separate architect, John Eveleigh, designed Somerset Place at about the same time, and the two crescents, with the two convex wings of Lansdown Place East and West, hug the hillside in a sinuous embrace. Cows and sheep still often graze in the fields immediately below, and beyond is the whole panorama of the city to Beechen Cliff south of the river. Mark Girouard noted this on a summer's evening, and commented on it in the introduction to his splendid book *The English Town*: "The cows munched, the houses hung still in the low sunlight; never had I seen such a sophisticated vision of how a town could be lived in. I had a sudden realization of a way of living in towns as enticing as it was sophisticated." Despite the addition of decorative ironwork, the architectural detail here is simpler than in earlier Georgian buildings—cost was a factor, but here location is everything.

Across the other side of Lansdown Road and a little further downhill is Camden Crescent, again probably by Eveleigh, with magnificent views across towards Bathampton. Even by Bath standards the slope is very steep indeed, and a large amount of vaulting and retaining walls were required to build here. Even so, the houses under construction at the far end of the crescent slipped during construction and were destroyed. We are left with a partial masterpiece, the central pediment with its Palladian columns but only four houses beyond it. Those who built on the slopes below Camden Crescent spent rather less care and money on their work. This was speculative building at its worst, and in the 1860s a series of landslips led to the demolition of the houses here. The result is one of Bath's prettiest parks—Hedgemead Park rather than the original name of Edgemead. Hedgemead Park, together with Henrietta Park in Bathwick, Alexandra Park on Beechen Cliff and the Royal Victoria Park, create as fine a quartet of public parks as one might wish for. And for those who like their parks to look rather more like parkland, there is always the National Trust's Prior Park Garden above Widcombe on the other bank of the Avon.

One ongoing problem with Bath terraces built on steep hillsides is the tension between the individual house with its individual string courses (or platbands) marking the division into storeys, and the idea of the terrace as a unified architectural composition. It was John Pinch the Elder who in the first decades of the nineteenth century solved this problem by making the platbands sweep up in unison from one house to the next. This makes a visit to Sydney Place on the Bathwick Estate, near the Holburne Museum, a must for those who want to discriminate between the very good, the ordinarily good and the rather average. The row was built storey by storey rather than house by house, using stone from the same quarry, with the platbands flowing up the gentle slope. A main cornice below the attic storey and a minor cornice above adopt the same graceful technique. Sydney Place has railed areas and balconies, but at Raby Place, at the bottom of Bathwick Hill, Pinch added the embellishment of covered balconies, giving a more Regency feel to the whole. Fans of Pinch will also want to visit Cavendish Place on the steep hillside next to the Approach Course (pitch-and-putt golf) where he used the same technique of ramping the string courses up from one house to the next. There is also Cavendish Crescent as if to show that this architect could match anything the Woods could manage.

Trade and Industry

The rise of Bath as a smart social and cultural centre in Georgian times was closely related to the growing spirit of economic enterprise in society. Transport improvements played a key part in opening it up to both visitors and to trade and industry. The first improvements were made to the roads, with the setting up of the Bath Turnpike Trust in 1708. By 1760 Bath was only two days' coach travel from London, and by 1830 less than a day away from the capital by stagecoach. London did business in London, but increasingly played in Bath, and the social connections made in Bath made their contribution in turn to business life back in London.

We have already seen that Ralph Allen was one of the moving spirits in establishing the Avon Navigation between Bristol and Bath, opened in 1727. This lowered the cost of goods being brought to the city from the region's greatest trade centre, and also the cost of opening up new markets for Bath stone. The Kennett and Avon Canal, climbing in a flight of locks from the River Avon at Widcombe and then passing through Sydney Gardens with a series of attractive over bridges in both stone and metal, made its own contribution, especially in the passage of bulk goods between Bath and Bristol in the west and London in the east. Underpinning at least some of the practical improvements in daily life was the development of a vibrant scientific life in Bath. The Bath Philosophical Society (1779-85) had no fewer than eleven members who were or later became Fellows of the Royal Society. Initially science was the province of aristocratic amateurs, but later men with more practical matters in mind, such as William Smith, surveyor of the Somerset Coal Canal and later dubbed the Father of English Geology, benefited from the intellectual atmosphere in Bath.

About 1800 everything began to go faster in Bath. Hard on the heels of the canals came the railways, and hard on the heels of Smith and his canal came the over-named Isambard Kingdom Brunel and his Great Western Railway. Brunel changed Bath in ways that Bath cannot have begun to suspect but which are still visible today. Brunel was in a hurry; the board of the GWR pressed Brunel; Brunel pressed his foremen; the foremen pressed the navvies. They died in their numbers, especially during the construction of Box Tunnel, where Brunel chose to strike dramatically due west from Chippenham to Bath rather than taking the more circuitous route through the Avon Valley. In Bath itself Brunel made the passage through Sydney Gardens, a pleasure ground where Jane Austen had enjoyed herself, with dramatic landscaping echoing the similar passage of the Kennett and Avon Canal a few years earlier. Brunel provided some Gothic decoration where the railway most closely approaches the urban centre near the Churchill Bridge that leads south out of the city centre, but he destroyed much of the ancient village of Twerton west of the city with a gaunt and monolithic viaduct. A new world had arrived. And it was a dirty world too. Those who remember Bath before the end of the steam era will agree: forget the golden light; most of Bath was at best grey, at worst, black. Bath stone and industrial pollution simply do not mix. Coal used by railway locomotives and burned in domestic hearths reacted with the limestone of the buildings, and produced a city which by mid-twentieth century was sooty and grimy, very unlike the gleaming World Heritage Site we admire today.

Some writers about Bath have tried to draw a clear line between what they describe as the "Georgian" city, allowing it perhaps to fade into the Regency style of the 1810s and 1820s, and the "industrial" city which they locate in the second half of the nineteenth century and the first half of the twentieth. This is wrong for at least two reasons. Firstly because history does not work like that, and all periods are more or less arbitrary. Secondly because the basis of the development of factory production in the nineteenth century was the economic boom of the eighteenth. Even before 1700, Bath was a popular resort. The visits of Anne of Denmark, wife of King James I, in 1602, 1613 and 1615 put Bath on the map as a spa city. In 1661 a spa water drinking fountain was set up. In addition to the home-based weaving industry, which had existed since the Middle Ages, there were milliners, drapers, bookbinders, brewers, grocers, doctors and bath attendants. What the eighteenth century did was to regulate Bath as a spa city, with rules for taking the waters and for polite society, thereby generating a demand for accommodation on an unprecedented scale. Population grew rapidly, in a way that most English towns did not experience until the 1800s. Three thousand in 1700 became ten thousand by 1760 and 30,000 by 1800. Those figures are for permanent residents and the figures including visitors would have been far higher.

Bath is fortunate in its Museum of Bath at Work, in the eccentric setting of an old indoor tennis court off Julian Road, somewhere above the Circus and the Assembly Rooms. This innovative museum explains the three stages of industrial development that were important to the growth of Georgian Bath. Most obviously there was construction, mainly in the form of speculative building, together with quarrying which provided the main building material. Then there was transport, as outlined above: roads, then canals, then railways. Finally there were service industries, providing jobs in domestic service, shops, inns and public houses, and laundry—not to mention the chairmen who carted visitors around in Sedan chairs (a little like Venetian gondoliers without the singing).

By the mid-twentieth century, Bath appeared to have lost much of its "special" character. Smoke-grimed, bomb-scarred, in the middle of a large programme of council house building, still sheltering the Admiralty which showed little sign of wanting to end its wartime evacuation, the city was trying hard to keep a smile on its face. An illustration in a 1948 guidebook shows Bath as a centre for the manufacture of tennis balls, Plasticine, Bath Oliver biscuits, cranes, invalid carriages, furniture, books and magazines, toys, corsets, dairy farming equipment and gauges. Firms such as Cross Manufacturing, Stothert & Pitt, Horstmann Gear Company and Rotork Controls were as much Bath as the abbey, the Georgian terraces, squares and crescents, and the Roman Baths. Visitors came, but for most Bathonians, it was a place to live and work much like any other town.

At the Museum of Bath at Work, it is possible to work through a series of local industries, following their development and importance to the city. As we shall see, many of these had their roots in the Georgian period or even earlier. The main development here is from a craft-based to a factory industry. The change was not always smooth, as the weaving industry shows. Towards the end of the eighteenth century, the Twerton mills specialized in the finishing processes for the already woven cloth. The Wiltshire weavers, especially at Bradford-on-Avon, were fiercely opposed to mechanization and the move to factory production, so cloth manufacturers found it easier to bring their cloth down to Twerton than to argue the point with their independent craftworkers. By 1787 feelings were running high and the Wiltshire weavers set out for Twerton. What they planned is unclear, but the authorities reacted very strongly. Magistrates called in troops in scenes re-enacted in the 1980s in the coalfields of Britain. Twerton survived and continued to manufacture cloth until the 1950s. Corset-making had existed in Bath in the eighteenth century but as a mass industry it arrived in 1891, and the red brick Bayer's Corset Factory took its place alongside Stothert & Pitt's foundry in the Lower Bristol Road. A familiar joke was that the two firms had much in common, both cranes and corsets having an uplifting effect.

Printing likewise has a long history in Bath, although in the twentieth-first century publishing and software development have the edge over book and magazine production. In the early 1800s there were no fewer than 150 printers of books, pamphlets and posters in the city, and printers were in the vanguard of the rise of radical Bath in the years before and after the Great Reform Act of 1832. But the family that came to dominate printing in Bath was that of Sir Isaac Pitman. Pitman was from an upwardly mobile non-conformist weaving family in Trowbridge, and Isaac began work in the mill at the age of twelve, as a junior clerk. He trained as a teacher and became a convert to Swedenborg's New Church. He invented shorthand. For the rest of his life shorthand, phonetics and the great cause of spelling reform were to dominate his life. Pitman reached Bath in 1839 and soon established his Phonetic Institute there, with printing as the commercial outlet for his new system of shorthand and his ideas on spelling reform.

Pitman's work is written into the fabric of the city, in Kingston Buildings on the south side of the abbey, where the fourth Phonetic Institute existed from 1874-79. The street name, carved into stone, is KIⱯSTON BILDIⱯZ. This is from the second stage of his spelling reform, with thirteen letters added to the standard alphabet. A later Pitman, Sir James, combined being MP for Bath in the mid-twentieth century with designing the Initial Teaching Alphabet (ITA) for young children learning to read and write. Sir James was a good Conservative, but the ITA was considered "trendy" and "progressive" and eventually discarded. And so the English still cannot spell their own language.

A number of industries exploited the numerous streams and springs of the Avon Valley, producing products for which there was a steady demand in the city. Water-driven paper mills developed from the eighteenth century, and in the nineteenth there were paper mills at Batheaston, Bathford, Weston Island and St. Catherine's. Off Summer Lane, between Combe Down and Monkton Combe, the De Montalt mill supplied a more specialist market for banknotes and artists' paper. Other local industries responded to the particular needs of Bath as a city of leisure and pleasure (or vice and immorality as others would have it). In 1735 Dr. William Oliver supplemented his income as a hospital physician by developing a recipe for digestive biscuits at his Green Street bakery—biscuits that could safely be eaten as part of taking the cure in Bath.

Bath in the eighteenth century became an important musical centre. Before William Herschel became an astronomer, he had come to Bath as organist and concert-promoter at the private Octagon chapel in Milsom Street. The organ which Herschel played was inaugurated in 1767 with a performance of Handel's *Messiah*. To support the musical life of Bath, instrument-makers, repairers, music shops and music teachers became established in the city. One of the most remarkable instrument-makers was William Sweetland. The first of his 300 organs was built for St. Michael's Church in the heart of Bath, and is still in weekly use. His career spanned the late 1840s until his retirement in 1902, centred on an organ factory originally built at the rear of his house in Cleveland Place West, a factory that existed until 1946. It was built like a church so as to imitate the acoustics of the religious buildings which were his best customers. In 1918 the firm was taken over by Duck, Son and Pinker, the Bath music shop founded at about the same time as Sweetland's factory.

Modern Times: the Battle for Bath

It will now be clear, I hope, that Bath is only in part a "Georgian" city. The Romans were here at Aquae Sulis for at least three hundred years. There was an important medieval city dominated by its great abbey and by the cloth industry. This "Cotswold" town gave way in turn to the Georgian city, and then a Victorian city in which leisure and pleasure were only part of a growing conurbation with a broad industrial base. In the twentieth century, and partly in response to bomb damage during the Second World War, Bath City Council built more houses than the whole total of eighteenth-century houses. They also built schools such as Newbridge Junior School to the west of the city. I went there when it was brand new, with its exposed metal beams, its hygienic cloakrooms and toilets, its large windows facing the south and the sun, a new world of health and vitality, and a remarkable contrast to the cramped, dark, little Victorian school (St. John's in the Upper Bristol Road) which I had previously attended. But in the main, the brave new world of 1950s primary schools is not what people come to Bath to see.

To many it seemed that post-war Bath was on a mission of self-destruction, seduced by some of the most unsavoury aspects of the modern world. In the main, modern Bath kept out of the city centre. It was when it began to encroach on that centre, and on to the Georgian housing north and west of the city centre that trouble erupted (perhaps a slow fuse would be a better metaphor). More will be said of these quarrels in Chapter 4, but I want to rehearse them here as they have affected what both resident and visitor experience today. The Second World War was the catalyst: Patrick Abercrombie produced his *Plan for Bath* in 1945. With its emphasis on individual set-piece buildings and relative lack of interest in the buildings that provided the settings for those recognized masterpieces, it set the tone for what followed. Abercrombie was not implemented, and Bath lost the chance of converting the Royal Crescent into a civic centre with a new council chamber at the rear. It also lost the idea of a concert hall on the site of pretty Abbey Green, a lack that still affects cultural life in the city.

After Abercrombie came Colin Buchanan with his plan to solve Bath's traffic problems with an east-west tunnel from Walcot Street to New King Street. This split the council on party lines (the Labour minority opposed it on social, financial and amenity grounds) but as a result, according to Fergusson and Mawl in their 1989 edition of

The Sack of Bath "Bath became a national, indeed an international scandal." There was massive planning blight at both ends of the tunnel but the plan remained still-born. What did get built was the Hilton Hotel in Walcot Street (and its attached multi-storey car-park), described by Michael Forsyth, not one to do violence through language, as "the most reviled building in Bath". And then there was Southgate Street, where there were problems, not least flooding. Boats and swans may be picturesque but do not really belong in a shopping street. A hotchpotch of buildings of dubious age was replaced by a shopping centre as graceless, formless and unpopular as any in the land. The twenty-first century has now completed a further redevelopment here, thus the second in my lifetime.

But Bath was on the move, slowly. The Bath Preservation Trust had been formed in 1934. Forsyth calculates that between 1950 and 1973 one thousand Georgian buildings, 350 of them listed, had been demolished (this in addition to the wartime losses). Following Abercrombie's lead, the "setting" of the acknowledged masterpieces had been thrown away, while the set pieces of the Circus, Royal Crescent and Assembly Rooms had been retained. All very well for those on their day trip from London, less good for the visitor who wanted to delve a little deeper into the treasures of Bath. This "Sack of Bath" (the title of the 1973 polemic by Adam Fergusson and Tim Mowl) hit the national headlines. Lord Snowdon came and took photos. John Betjeman, who had lived in Bath during the war, came and mourned. Bath was a national treasure, they argued, not to be left in the hands of untrustworthy local politicians and their electors.

Things change, conservation became the new good. The conservationists, closely allied to the tourist industry, won the battle of Bath. In this new Bath nothing must be altered, everything must shine, all development must be resisted. Some wondered if this process might have gone too far. A loud public campaign for the electricity showrooms in Dorchester Street claimed to protect a rather poor example of 1920s neoclassicism. They lost that one, and Bath gained its cheerful and rather efficient new bus-station—the "busometer" (by architectural analogy with gasometer which part of it closely resembles). It faces cheekily across Dorchester Street the monstrous neo-neoclassical film-set of the new Southgate Street shopping centre. Other *causes célèbres* included the saga of the non-arrival of the Dyson School of Engineering Design which was to replace the Newark Works of Stothert & Pitt, sold down the river in the late 1980s.

Tread softly in Bath: there is much history under your feet, and many sensitivities too.

THE URBAN MAP

Thermae Bath Spa

3 | Landmarks
Buildings, Streets and Styles

In this chapter, which looks at the architectural highlights of the city, I concentrate on those sites easily accessible on foot within central Bath. In the main they are within the area defined by the old medieval city walls, and places immediately adjacent such as Kingsmead Square, Milsom Street, Walcot Street and Pulteney Bridge and Street. Better-known but slightly distant streets, such as the Royal Crescent and Circus, have already been described in Chapter 2 as part of the growth of eighteenth-century Bath.

Kingsmead Square

Kingsmead Square is Bath on the cusp, between ancient and modern, lovely and hideous, the personal and the public. Let me begin with the personal. Nowadays Kingsmead Square is pretty much pedestrian-only; fifty years ago it was the bus-stop for coming home from the town centre on a Saturday morning—those same Saturday morning expeditions that involved drinking the evil-smelling spa water from the public fountain in Stall Street. The square was dominated by an enormous plane-tree that seemed to stretch from one side to the other and heavenwards far above our childish heads and far above the roof of the double-decker bus we were clambering aboard. Well, that plane-tree is still there, it survives, it is still enormous, it is well cared for by the Council Parks Department, carries pretty lights at Christmas and shelters a frequent fruit and vegetable stall beneath its limbs. How calm and stately in winter, how green and sprightly in spring, how welcoming its shade in summer, how mournful its dead leaves and flaking bark in autumn.

The dominant building in Kingsmead Square is undoubtedly Rosewell House, famously condemned by John Wood as "nothing save ornaments without taste", in a rather strange decorative style that Michael Forsyth describes as "provincial Baroque". The architect was Nathaniel Ireson of Wincanton in south-east Somerset. Wood's anger stemmed from the fact that he had already begun work on Queen Square and was determined to impose his new classical style on the city. Certainly the building fits oddly with the elegant south side of the square, not by Wood but already recognizably Georgian. The façade was lovingly restored in the 1970s after the publication of Adam Ferguson and Tim Mawl's *Sack Of Bath*. But it was a close-run thing.

Provincial and architectural hotchpotch Rosewell House may be, but it has survived. Far worse than Rosewell House itself, which I rather like, is the view past the house. This was a bomb-site after the Second World War, but both the housing (Rosewell Court) and office developments clearly visible here are of poor quality and will no doubt need further "redevelopment" at a later date. Kingsmead Square has no east side and there is a clear view along Westgate Street towards the city centre, with the Abbey tower just visible.

From the north-east corner, another view opens towards the Theatre Royal and its neighbour, Beau Nash's house. More will be said about this when we trace the history of Bath's theatrical life. The still rather open and neglected-looking area in front is the Sawclose. From its early beginnings as timber-yard and saw-pit within the city-walls, it seems to have developed as a place for a range of messy activities not deemed appropriate to more select corners of the city. In recent years a garage, car-park and theatre-turned-bingo-hall have all fitted comfortably into this space. The whole is dominated by the High Victorian building known as Bluecoat House, with its Jacobean chimneys and clock-tower. From the early eighteenth century there was indeed a "blue coat" school on this site, named of course after the uniform worn by the children. John Wood the Elder was one of its pupils.

Pulteney Bridge and Pulteney Street

The view of Pulteney Bridge from the Grand Parade is one of the most photographed in Bath, but also one of special significance for the author. The key is the little building sandwiched between the entrance to the covered market and the Victoria Art Gallery which was once the Children's Library. Going into the library to change books was part of my childhood ritual of Saturday mornings in Bath, and was always followed by crossing the road to view the Pulteney Bridge from the smart and polished side and the River Avon, brown and wild in flood, calm and green in quieter seasons. Of course it has changed: the straight weir angled out from one bank to the other has been replaced by a sharply convex weir and a sluice gate which has protected most of Bath from flooding for nearly fifty years now. Once there were mills, now there are pleasure grounds. It remains the most iconic view in the city, and I for one can see why.

Pulteney Bridge is famous for two reasons. Firstly, because it is as original and exciting a structure as any in the city. Secondly, it is one of a tiny number of bridges in Europe with shops on both sides. Pulteney Bridge was the work of the eighteenth-century designer and architect Robert Adam, curiously the only example of his work in Bath. He submitted a grandiose design for the Upper Assembly Rooms, but it was dismissed as too expensive. He began work on the palatial prison (now converted into flats) in Grove Street but was replaced by Thomas Attwood. The Grand Parade view above the weir shows off the two mid-stream piers and the large Venetian window beneath the central pediment. Time has been less good to the northern face of the bridge, which was rebuilt by John Pinch the Elder, when one of the piers collapsed in 1800. It has acquired various box-like timber structures hanging on as if for life itself, rather like the similarly fated Ponte Vecchio in Florence. This has become more visible in recent years, with the opening up of the Podium and the riverside walk on the west bank and tidying up in Grove Street where there is a good view of the prison.

On the south side of the bridge, one of the longest-serving shops is the Bath Stamp and Coin Shop. This began life in the pedestrian alley called Northumberland Place (see below) and moved the short distance down the road in 1958. It is currently owned by the son of the Mr. and Mrs. Swindell who began the business. As a small boy, I was a customer of theirs, and can swear that their name was a complete misnomer; I always found them honest and kind, and keen to make my pocket-money stretch as far as possible.

Across Pulteney Bridge we are still in shopping Bath and it is not immediately obvious that this is the beginning of the very extensive Bathwick estate stretching down the length of Pulteney Street to the Holburne Museum and beyond. The Bathwick estate, east of the River Avon, was purchased by William Pulteney in 1727 and developed as an up-market residential area between then and the end of the eighteenth century. The Recreation Ground, the current home of Bath Rugby, lies close at hand, and their merchandise shop is here too. And among the shops is the fine Argyll Street United Reform Church (originally Congregational). This is one of H. E. Goodridge's exercises in Greek Revival, extended from an earlier building in the nineteenth century. It is a building that speaks of the self-confidence and vigour of non-conformity in a city where the word non-conformist is not the first that comes to mind. Inside it is lovely indeed, with a large balcony supported on slender metal columns, fine if subdued coloured glass and a lot of yellow paint. There is an imposing preaching dais full centre with an organ by the Bath organ-maker William Sweetland behind; a modest clock on the balcony will remind the preacher that a speaker's words may be better judged by their depth rather than their length. Like several such buildings in Bath it has proved a happy home for the early spring literary festival, although to my knowledge no speaker has yet dared to ascend the pulpit. One curious relic here is the pump which was kept in the basement and used to raise water from an underground well. Bath springs eternal.

At Laura Place, a diamond-shaped open space with a central fountain, the vista widens out. To the south Johnstone Street offers a free view of the rugby pitch on the Recreation Ground, and the spire of St. John's Church and Beechen Cliff beyond. At a different angle, one looks back to the southern end of the Bathwick estate and the Bath Skyline at Claverton Down. To the north side of Laura Place, Henrietta Street was the home of the Laura Chapel from 1795, one of Bath's elegant little private chapels (though this one held 1000 people). It is no longer, though the name remains on the wall.

Beyond Laura Place we are into the grandiose and slightly sad architecture of Pulteney Street, the main thoroughfare of the Bathwick estate—sad because at most times of day and on most days of the year, it is so vast and so empty. Great Pulteney Street (although Bathonians seldom bother with the well-justified Great) is 1,100 feet long and one hundred feet wide. With rusticated ground floors, mansard roofs and railed basements to the street front, this is pretty standard late Georgian and Regency speculative building. The whole of this Bathwick estate was designed by Thomas Baldwin (with additional work by John Pinch). Forsyth's Pevsner guide describes it as "a departure from the standard Palladian style of John Wood's successors towards the new and fashionable neoclassical style of Robert Adam—axial, geometric and large scale". Over the years, the apartments and houses of Pulteney Street have had many famous residents. We might note for example William Smith, who worked on the Somerset Coal Canal in the valleys south of Bath, and held earnest conversations at Bath's Royal Literary and Scientific Institution, or Hannah More, whose plays were performed at Bath's Theatre Royal and who later set up schools in villages in North Somerset with a view to saving the souls of the hard-pressed local peasantry. And her friend and fellow social reformer William Wilberforce, whose name is inextricably linked with the abolition of the pernicious slave trade on which so much of the wealth of Bath and Bristol is based.

The vista at the east end of Pulteney Street is closed by the Holburne Museum, designed at the same time as the pleasure grounds of Sydney Gardens. This dates from the last years of the eighteenth century. The Sydney Hotel was intended as a Janus building, with a formal façade facing down Pulteney Street and a more informal exterior opening out onto the pleasure gardens. The ground floor contained tea, coffee and card rooms, with a ballroom above. The establishment did not thrive for long. Bath was past its heyday as a social centre, becoming more settled, duller if you will, entering its middle-age as a city. Soon the gardens would be threaded by first the Kennett and Avon Canal, and later by the Great Western Railway. The rear was modified and lost its sense of belonging to the gardens. Changes of use were frequent, until in the twentieth century it acquired a new use as the home for the Holburne of Menstrie art collection. At the same time, the building was modified and lost its wings in favour of the two present colonnades. As an art gallery it has proved, to say the least, difficult to manage. We shall have more to say about the Holburne later in this book ...

The Guildhall

There is nowhere that defines Bath quite so well as the enclosed space of the High Street and Northgate Street, dominated by the gothic abbey to the south, the classical Guildhall and its extension to the east, and the fine Victorian neo-gothic spire of St. Michael's to the north. This is a very different impression of the abbey from that obtained in the Abbey Churchyard, where the vertical dominates. Here in the High Street it is the glazed length of the nave that helps to give breadth to this particular streetscape, reminding us that this would have been in medieval times the open market place where church and town met (as they still do in Wells, where an open-air market graces the space before the cathedral and bishop's palace). There is also the soaring glass elevation of the north transept with its clock right at the apex, which serves to define as closely as possible Bath time.

The east side of the High Street is the Guildhall, with a satisfy-ing classical façade by Thomas Baldwin. Inside the building reflects the importance the Corporation attached to entertaining distin-guished visitors, holding formal banquets and so on. In an age rightly concerned with sleaze and strict economy in local government, en-tertainment is now generally confined to the Mayor's Parlour, al-though Queen Elizabeth II was entertained to lunch there on her jubilee visit in 2002. So the richly decorated Banqueting Hall on the first floor, with its fine chandeliers, finds alternative uses, especially for recitals during the International Music Festival in June, and writers talking about their work during the Bath Literature Festival in March. Indeed, the Literature Festival rather lives in the Guildhall, with a smaller second hall for more informal talks, a café and a book-stall. One of the most charming rooms in the Guildhall is the

Mayor's Parlour, with its Arthurian round table, where he or she continues to entertain official guests. It is not normally open to members of the public, except that is during Heritage Open Week or if you have a particular wish to get married there. The parlour is located in the southern Victorian extension, together with the Council chamber and committee rooms.

Bath is one of a number of towns and cities which have acquired trustee status. It is therefore able to continue with its mayoral traditions despite local government reorganization and unitary authorities. So thirty-two of the sixty-five members of Bath and North-East Somerset Council constitute the Charter Trustees, with the mayor as Chair. Famous mayors have included Ralph Allen in 1742 and in 1826 Eleazer Pickwick. Pickwick was the landlord of the White Hart Inn, and well known to Charles Dickens. It is probable that Dickens used not only the name but the rotund joviality of mine host as his model in *Pickwick Papers*. A number of paintings from the Victoria Art Gallery will be found hanging on the Guildhall walls, including two of Allen, and a portrait of George III by Sir Joshua Reynolds. From 1954 until their theft, there were two elephant tusks in the corridor outside the Mayor's Parlour, a gift to the city by the Emperor of Ethiopia, Haile Selassie, who spent his years of exile, 1936-41, in Bath.

Forsyth raises an interesting issue about the flamboyance of the Guildhall being a riposte by the tradespeople of Bath to the extravagance of the new Assembly Rooms, from which some of them were excluded for social reasons, even though they were important civic dignitaries. The side wings of the Guildhall are late Victorian additions, as is the Victoria Art Gallery round the corner in Bridge Street. Through the north wing of the Guildhall is an entrance to the covered market, a cheerful corner of the city and a nice reminder of the practical concerns of the Cotswold market-town that preceded Georgian Bath and the workaday Victorian/modern town that succeeded it.

Nosing around at the back of buildings in Bath can lead to some unpleasant shocks because so often all the effort and money have gone into the façade alone. At the Guildhall, the inquisitive are in for a pleasant surprise because here it reveals the light and elegant rear elevation, and maybe the gleam of those extravagant and mesmerizing chandeliers in the ballroom on the first floor. From the same vantage point it is also possible to admire the outside of the present-day little covered market, for all the world like some Turkish mosque. Another pleasant surprise in the Guildhall, once you have got past the security staff, is the Bath Record Office in the basement, a goldmine for local historians and family historians presided over for some years past by the genial Colin Johnston.

Bath Street

Bath Street is where heritage Bath began. But let us wind back a little further to its origins. Bath Street is a fine example of municipal enterprise, and Bath Corporation knew how to use parliamentary procedures to tackle urban renewal. The Bath Act of 1789 led to the building of Bath Street with its colonnades on both sides and subtle crescent-shaped widenings at both ends, as satisfying and formal a streetscape as any in Bath. The Corporation had estimated the cost at £73,000 of which £42,000 could be recovered by sale of building plots. In the event, the cost was £64,000 and the income £51,000, so the improvements cost the city little new money. Modern politicians still grappling with the finances of the spa building, the entrance to which is in one of the western widenings, can only reflect with wonderment at their Georgian predecessors. In fact, of course, it did not work as easily as that. The 1789 Act was based on plans by City Surveyor Thomas Baldwin but the financial crisis generated by the French Wars bankrupted Baldwin and led to the failure of the Bath Bank in 1793. The new Pump Room and Bath Street did get built, although other improvements had to wait until the arrival of the new century.

The view is closed at both ends: at the western end by the Cross Bath with St. John's Hospital behind it; at the eastern end by the screen of columns with pediment above that formed the entrance to the Private Baths (now the entrance to the Roman Baths Museum) with the Pump Room and abbey behind. Baldwin had designed, only a few years before, a new façade, decorative and curvaceous, but north-facing, for the Cross Bath. But once Bath Street had been built, it was obvious that this did not fit the new street alignment. It was left to Baldwin's successor, John Palmer, to rebuild Baldwin's front so that it now faced east along the colonnaded street. The Cross Bath has seen many vicissitudes, but is now beautifully restored as part of the new spa complex. Where Grimshaw's New Royal Bath is the throbbing social centre of the whole, and John Wood's Hot Bath its medical centre, the Cross Bath, small but perfect, is without doubt its spiritual centre, a moment of calm and peace in the busy twenty-first-century city.

That Bath Street has survived is a story in itself. In their book on the 1909 Pageant, Elliott and Swift recount the drama of the "Wake up, Bath!" campaign of the same year. This rehearsed many of the arguments that were to recur in Bath in the second half of the century, the focus being the balance between Bath for the Bathonians and Bath for the visitors. The Battle of Bath Street was central to "Wake up Bath!" The detail is beside the point here, and as in most Bath battles, very detailed indeed. The Corporation produced a plan to modernize that involved the rebuilding of the north side of Bath Street and the destruction of the north colonnade and therefore the symmetry of the street.

One of the professional consultants used by the Corporation was Frederick Bligh Bond, later notorious as the man in charge of excavations at Glastonbury Abbey, which he conducted in accordance with his own rather bizarre spiritualist beliefs. He reported that the premises "hardly appear of a nature to repay renovation". Eventually the plans were quietly shelved, but the lasting legacy of 1909 was the formation of the Old Bath Preservation Society and the beginnings of a more systematic approach to the preservation of Bath's architectural heritage. As for Bath Street, it has remained more or less intact, against the odds, despite the demolition of the Pump Room Hotel which stood on Stall Street immediately opposite the Abbey Churchyard and the removal of the municipal baths stretching behind the street front along the north side of Bath Street. Now a large chain store inhabits the buildings, but the splendid façade and the colonnades still bear witness to the vigour of municipal enterprise in late Georgian Bath.

Abbey Green

Abbey Green lies south of the abbey, in a tiny area of old streets and lanes suggestive of pre-Georgian Bath, but that butts onto the modern shopping area stretching south to the river and the railway and bus stations. There, beneath the spreading shade of a great old plane-tree, lies a close, cosy world, largely untroubled by the uncertainties and insecurities of the twentieth and twenty-first centuries. Yet Abbey Green is protected from intrusions by one of the few pieces of twentieth-century classicism of which this author approves wholeheartedly: St. Michael's Arch. A flattened archway with offices above, it gives a satisfying sense of closure here, and only the camera that never lies will spot the words Marks and Spencer engraved on the wall beyond. Unfortunately, that great Bath institution Fishy Evans' fish-and-chip shop and café, which lay immediately beyond the arch on the left, has not survived into the new century. It is remembered fondly by several generations of older Bathonians, especially old boys of Bath Technical School which until the 1960s was still in the city centre. One old boy of Kingswood School, the Methodist boarding-school on Lansdown, told me how he and his friends would escape on a Saturday afternoon to watch Bath City play football at Twerton Park, and then return via Fishy Evans' for supper. It was a round trip of six or seven miles on foot, with the saved bus-fares paying for the supper.

All the buildings in Abbey Green repay careful attention, preferably with Forsyth's architectural guide in hand. It comes as something of a surprise to discover that the two-storey Crystal Palace pub was once a three-storey Georgian building. It is one of the few buildings in central Bath that has been rendered and painted. Its 2011 colour scheme was bright yellow with architectural details picked out in green and the pub name in red. Above it, the "Greek" chimney of the old City Laundry (more municipal enterprise) appears to sprout from its roof-top. Opposite and at the other extreme of heritage Bath is no. 3, a late seventeenth-century house with gables above. The stone-work, much rougher than the ashlar blocks used by the Georgian builders for their façades, suggests that this was probably once rendered as well. West-facing, it has those evening honey tones that immediately make one think of the Cotswolds. Abbey Green is a place to linger and look, whether your tastes run to beer from the Crystal Palace, sweets from the Bath Sweetshop or beads from the shop next door to the pub.

Milsom Street

Milsom Street, sloping gently from north to south, has retained some of its status as Bath's smartest shopping street. As at Bath Street, the Corporation was the major player here. It was the landowner and shared the risk of the development (from 1761 onwards) with the title and profits eventually reverting to the Corporation. Municipal enterprise was not invented in Bath but certainly benefited the city. The building of the east side includes the five palatial houses known as Somersetshire Buildings, and these imposing buildings lend a grandeur to the whole street which has stood the test of time, not to mention the arrival of Jamie's Italian restaurant somewhere behind the shop fronts in the new venture known as Milsom Place. In later years, Milsom Street doubled with the High Street as a venue for processions and national celebrations. As late as 1909, when the Duke of Connaught visited the Bath Pageant in the Royal Victoria Park, and travelled in procession from the Guildhall to the park, the passage of Milsom Street was a highlight. In their monumental and exhaustive book on the pageant, Kirsten Elliott and Andrew Swift quote the description of a journalist: "The people of... Milsom Street have thrown aside the reverential restraint of age, and decorated their houses and shops with splendid hues that recall the joyous days when the uncrowned King of Bath (Beau Nash rather than Bladud) drove along those thoroughfares in his gaudy chariot..." and so on. The Milsom Street development began in 1761, Nash died in 1761, but when was truth an obstacle to good journalism?

The oldest of the smart shops in Milsom Street is Jolly's (now part of House of Fraser), which opened its "Bath Emporium" as early as 1831. The "Bath in Time" on-line photographic collection features a number of views of Milsom Street, still recognizable today. They include a 1920s photo featuring luxury motor-cars waiting patiently for their owners outside Jolly's, while a solitary pony and trap marks the world that is disappearing. The store occupies nearly half the western side, with Waterstone's bookshop next door, and a range of clothes and household goods shops. There are banks, although the two at the top of the street have both become restaurants. No doubt there are people who enjoy dining in these rather elegant and echoing old banking halls. Culpeper the herbalist has a shop here, as does Highgrove, which markets various products connected with the Prince of Wales' estate at (you guessed it) Highgrove.

Northumberland Place

Opposite the Guildhall is a pretty unsuccessful twentieth-century exercise in mock unadorned Georgian complete with mock mansard roof. This used to be the well-known Bath grocery store of Cater, Stoffell and Fortt. It is sometimes known as the Harvey's building, as the Bristol sherry firm took over the store before passing it on for that evil activity known as property development. They should have stuck to sherry.

The most attractive features on this side of the High Street are the Corridor and Northumberland Place, both pedestrian shopping arcades but completely different in character. The Corridor, built in 1825 as a venture by the young H. E. Goodridge, is closed and narrow and permanently illuminated, with a wider opening to the High Street supported by two marble columns. Northumberland Place is open to the air, flower-filled in summer and boasts one of Bath's best small pubs, the Coeur-de-Lion. Anyone familiar with the Bath version of the Somerset dialect of English will appreciate why locals call it The Cur. The entrance to the Place from the High Street is narrow and gives little indication of the pleasures to be discovered inside.

The traders of Northumberland Place have been working for half a century at creating a pedestrian shopping experience that is, well, different. Rickard's, the bag and luggage shop at the corner of Union Passage, is one of the oldest shops. Simon Rogers' father acquired the business many years ago and decided to keep the name, which was that of a local manufacturer of leather luggage. Simon and I both remember Eileen's garden shop which used to be next door, with trays of plants laid out on wooden benches in front. Now the traders meet informally to make sure the Place is kept "interesting and independent" in the words of Elaine Rogers. They work with the Council to ensure extra flowers along the street; the bunting is still up from a summer party with live music, and will only come down in time for the Christmas decorations to go up. A plaque remembers Leslie's Menswear, the dreamchild of Leslie Towers and his business partner Dermot Parnell, and the first shop in Bath to stock jeans. The plaque continues: "Along this path Leslie and Dermot showed retail Bath the power of flowers. 1960-87."

The Hilton Hotel and Walcot Street

Above the junction with Bridge Street, High Street becomes the wild jumble of Northgate Street. On the right is a music shop. The shop-front says Milsom and Son, a company established in 1825. Another music firm with the romantic and aquatic name of Duck Son and Pinker was established in 1848, and the two companies merged as early as 1878. Their closure in 2011 brings to an end nearly 200 years of Bath's musical history. Nearby is Slippery Lane, Bath's only surviving medieval lane, which led down to the ferry replaced by Pulteney Bridge. To the right again is the Podium shopping centre, incorporating the library and a supermarket. Rather than gaze on these buildings, it is better to raise the eyes above Walcot Street towards the trees of Hedgemead Park, Camden Crescent, and the tower of St. Stephen's Lansdown, its neo-gothic tower complementing the spire of George Philip Manners' St. Michael's which is sandwiched between the entrances to Broad Street and Walcot Street. Inside it is warm and inviting but for the moment we must stay outside.

The greatest praise that one can heap on the Podium, built in 1987-89, is that is obscures and draws attention away from the blank-faced non-architecture of the Hilton Hotel and its associated car-park, dating from 1972. Cities like Bath can be fierce places to live and work, especially if you want to set up a small business, or do something a bit different from mainstream retailing. Yet cities can provide opportunities in the most unlikely way. In the late 1960s

Colin Buchanan devised a plan to solve the notorious Bath traffic problem by constructing a tunnel under the city centre. That tunnel was to have emerged somewhere in the vicinity of Walcot Street. The tunnel was never built, but curiously the car-park and hotel were.

During the years of debate Walcot Street and the yards and side turnings between the street and the river went into decline. But from that decline there emerged a different kind of culture and a different kind of business, taking advantage of the fact that no-one else wanted to be in Walcot. What was bad news for the city was good news for a whole wave of alternatives from the Bath Fringe Festival to the remarkably successful Walcot Reclamation. Two key buildings that otherwise might have been demolished—the Tramshed and the Corn Market—were saved to rise again with the new century. Work continues on the Corn Market, but the Tramshed, with its glazed tile exterior, once the humming hub of Bath's electric tram network, has been cleverly converted to flats orientated towards the river with a bar and grill fronting onto the street. Amid so much change, another great survivor is the Bell Inn, still a popular pub and music venue, famous in the 1960s for its jazz and still famous for its jazz, with some blues, rock and country music thrown in for good measure.

Ralph Allen's Town House

Seek and you will find. Of no building in central Bath is this truer than Ralph Allen's town house. If Prior Park was his business headquarters, then this much smaller mansion was home. To find it, first locate the Quaker Meeting-House in York Street, not the humble, unassuming building you might expect from this gentle sect, but a giant of a building with four fluted Ionic columns supporting a pediment, Bath's strictest study in early nineteenth-century Greek Revival. This mysterious conjunction of Quakers and Greek Revival is easily solved—this was built not for the Quakers but for the Masons. By squeezing up against the right-hand corner of the meeting-house (the modern entrance) there is an oblique view of Ralph Allen's house, now almost completely surrounded by other, later buildings.

The house was built as an extension in 1727 to an earlier house in North Parade Passage, a couple of doors down from Sally Lunn's tea-rooms. The passage was once called Lilliput Alley in recognition of its narrowness, and runs parallel to York Street from Abbey Green to Terrace Walk. The extension is at right angles to the house in the passage. It is usually attributed to Wood the Elder, though he never claimed the design. Certainly it is richer, more elaborate than any of his other work in Bath, a graceful narrow Roman temple, with four Corinthian columns and elaborately decorated pediment. The only other view to be had of the house is down the narrow passage next to the Huntsman pub, which happens to be the entrance to its beer-cellar. At one time, Allen would have had a view to Sham Castle on Bathampton Down—indeed, the main purpose of Sham Castle was to provide a view from Allen's house—but more recent buildings have cut off the view.

Bog Island

The Pump Room and the Assembly Rooms were the places where the set of rules for polite social intercourse, laid down by Master of Ceremonies Beau Nash, were most carefully observed. The original Assembly Rooms were in the city centre, though later in the eighteenth century they were supplemented by the new or Upper Rooms, near the Circus. By 1800 this vision was fading, and parties and social gatherings were increasingly private affairs, held in private houses or apartments in the city. In 1820 the Lower Rooms in Terrace Walk burned down, and there was no call to replace them. Instead, the site was rebuilt in 1825 to house what was to become the Bath Royal Literary and Scientific Institution (BRLSI), where men (and a few women) planned the shape of the future. Like its near neighbour— the Masonic Hall turned Quaker meeting-house in York Street—it was overstated Greek Revival by William Wilkins. Then in 1933 the building was demolished to allow for road widening, and the BRLSI moved to Queen Square where it continues to promote science and the humanities alike.

Soon the triangular space that remained was to acquire the less-than-flattering name of Bog Island, playing host to underground toilets. Now the toilets themselves (that is, the bogs) have gone and the Bath water fountain, now dry, moved here from Stall Street. Yet even the toilets had an afterlife. A number of Bath Rugby players including Cornishman Roger Spurrell and Scottish international Damian Cronin, established a nightclub here in the 1980s, using fellow players as bouncers. Oh for those days of amateur rugby on the nearby Rec! Such, then, is the recent curious histor

The Guildhall before the addition of the Victorian extensions

4 | **Rulers and Ruled**
A Brief Social and Political History

> "Society in every state is a blessing, but government is but a necessary evil; in its worst state an intolerable one; for when we suffer, or are exposed to the same miseries by a government, which we might expect in a country without government, our calamities are heightened by reflecting that we furnish the means by which we suffer. Government, like dress, is the badge of lost innocence; the palaces of kings are built on the ruins of the bowers of paradise."
>
> Tom Paine, *Common Sense* (1776)

1776 was a critical year in British history. It was also to become a critical year in the history of the United States of America, the year of the Declaration of Independence and the opening shots of the War of Independence. Georgian Bath was at the height of its fame as the destination of preference of the rich and cultured. It was also the year in which Tom Paine published *Common Sense*, to be followed in 1791/2 by *The Rights of Man*. In the one he justifies the American Revolution, in the other the French Revolution.

Revolutionaries are dangerous men. In the last quarter of the eighteenth century the political classes were either for or against Paine. Sitting on fences, philosophical or actual, was not an option. Three of his most determined opponents—William Pitt the Younger (prime minister), Edmund Burke (trenchant critic of the French Revolution and other such democratic innovations) and Hannah More (conservative, evangelical do-gooder)—have blue memorial plaques in Pulteney Street and Laura Place. By contrast, Tom Paine suffered the indignity of being burned in effigy on Beechen Cliff during the winter of 1792/3. Bath was not the only town where he burned, but it had special reason to dislike Paine, who had attacked the abuses of the privileges granted by charter to many of England's cities. In *The Rights of Man* he argued that corporations actually limited the rights of citizens by excluding the majority from key privileges such as the election of Members of Parliament.

In this chapter we have landed, somewhat dramatically, in the heart of a political debate that can be extended both backwards and forwards from those pivotal years of the 1790s. It is both a debate internal to the city—the relationship between citizens and their ruling Corporation—and a wider debate about how it related to the rest of the country and the national body politic. Perhaps an earlier starting-point may help to demonstrate what was at stake then, while by carrying the arguments forward into the present, we can better understand how rulers and ruled relate to one another in contemporary Bath.

The Corporation

Much of medieval Bath, including the water-mills, was controlled by the abbey. With the sale of church property at the Reformation, it was far from clear who would take responsibility for the regulation of markets, of the crafts, of the weaving industry, of the already popular spa waters. Elizabeth I resolved the issue fifty years later in 1590 by issuing the city with a charter. This meant the city would be run by a small group of councillors and aldermen. They had the power to select their own members, to select two members of the national parliament and to exercise justice within the city. New councillors might be chosen from among the freemen of the city but were not elected by the freemen or responsible to them. From the start, Bath, like Venice, was an oligarchy. Unlike that city state, Bath had to take account of wider national developments.

The Corporation's power, like that of the pre-Reformation abbey, derived from the ownership of most of the property within the city walls. As private citizens, members of the Corporation also owned property, especially inns. An impressive Guildhall was the external badge of their authority, although as we have seen, only the figures of King Cole and King Bladud lodged in Bath Street are evidence of the existence of such a pre-Georgian building. During the Civil War period Bath opted to support the parliamentary cause, but the argument, as in much of the country, was an argument within a social class, both within the city and in the countryside beyond. There was indeed a great swell of popular feeling going on within the parliamentary army, the non-conformist sects, the independent craftsmen, but this was more the backdrop to the action than the action itself, which was led by men of property such as Alexander Popham, one of Bath's two members of parliament. At the same time, this popular sentiment in favour of the Protestant religion, the local against the national, sober hard work against lavish display, made sure that many rallied to the call of arms once the Civil War had started in 1642.

Under royalist control from 1643-45, Bath submitted, whatever the loyalties of Corporation and townsfolk alike. John Wroughton, whose splendid study of the Civil War in Bath and North Somerset has informed my own reflections on this period, wrote:

> For the next two years local people submitted to their new rulers with a sullen sense of inevitability. There was no underground resistance movement, no sabotage and no acts of heroic defiance. They concentrated instead on maintaining the flow of daily life, farming their fields, weaving their cloths and keeping open their markets. The Bath Corporation continued to meet, as it did throughout the war, royalist and parliamentarian sympathisers sitting together side by side to ensure that the local economy survived and that essential business was not neglected.

As so often, the Corporation was guided more by its own sense of economic interest than by any ideological motivation. From 1645 the position was reversed, and the Corporation dominated by a faction sympathetic to Cromwell's Commonwealth. The traditionalist (royalist) faction under Henry Chapman continued to argue for such traditional English delights as bear-baiting, reflecting that sense that the Puritans had suppressed the popular festivities summed up in the phrase "Merrie England". Nevertheless, Wroughton concedes that after the 1660 Restoration of King Charles II, Chapman was eventually a popular mayor who advertised Bath waters in the London press (1664), wrote a book about their healing properties

(*Thermae Redivivae*, 1673) and laid the foundations for the Golden Age of Georgian Bath.

The backwash of the seventeenth-century maelstrom of religion and politics came with the reign of the openly Roman Catholic James II, the unsuccessful and bloodily repressed Monmouth Rebellion of 1685 (remembered around Bath as the "Pitchfork Rebellion") and the replacement of James in 1688 by the Protestant monarchs William and Mary, prepared at least to work with parliament to rule the country. Bath had a certain business interest in all this. It was widely believed that James II's wife, Mary of Modena, a devout Catholic, had conceived following a visit to take the spa waters in Bath. This was good publicity, and Bath Corporation sent a number of loyal addresses to James to congratulate him on the birth of a legitimate heir. Poor Mary is remembered for that fact only— that she gave birth to a legitimate son and heir. Once it was clear that the Protestants William and Mary were going to take the throne, the Corporation, anxious to welcome the new dispensation, voted to remove "the Crowne of Thorns in the Cross Bath and the cross thereon and all superstitious things belonging thereunto". The only known victim was the Catholic Master of King Edward's Grammar School, appointed by King James in 1687. He was supplanted neatly and speedily by the very man he had replaced.

The Grammar School was to recur in the political history of Bath. In 1734 the Master, concerned at the financial state of the school, translated the original endowment documents. It became obvious that the Corporation, trustees of the school, had been salting away for years the money that belonged by right to the school. The Master took them to court, and the Corporation was condemned for its corruption. This brings us to the nub of debates about the Corporation. The more fashionable Bath became, the higher property prices and rents rose, and the richer the Corporation became. In the mid-Georgian period, as we have seen, it erected a magnificent new Guildhall, classically sober on the outside but lavishly opulent within. Plans for the new Guildhall had been drawn up in 1760. They were opposed by Thomas Attwood who wanted the contract for himself. Finally in 1775 he got his way, but died in a site accident shortly after. So it was his assistant Thomas Baldwin who took on design and construction.

For a moment, we will return to national matters. In 1715 Bath was occupied by a military force under General Wade, as security against a possible Jacobite rising in the West Country. No such rising against the new Hanoverian dynasty took place, but from 1722-47 Bath elected Wade as one of its MPs. In 1722 the Corporation elected Ralph Allen, quarryman entrepreneur, onto its General Council. In 1745, with Wade away suppressing the 1745 Jacobite rising, it was Ralph Allen who raised a scratch force in the city and paraded it before the Guildhall. Later it was Wade who oversaw the Scottish Highland clearances and the building of roads through the region which would ensure that never again would England's peace be disturbed by its northern neighbour Scotland. Well, that was the aim.

Bath was now firmly in the mainstream of eighteenth-century politics, and Bath Corporation was certainly proactive in facilitating the development of the late Georgian city through the 1766 and 1789 Acts of Parliament. But the second of these two acts also suggests the way that Corporation activities were limited by wider economic considerations, in this case the effect of the French wars on the economy and the availability of finance, so that many of the improvements enabled by the 1789 Act were not in fact completed until the new century. The situation was not helped by the fact that the Act had established a board of Improvement Commissioners—54 in all, with a quorum of only five. As R. S. Neale points out in his exhaustive history of the city at this period, it was scarcely an administrative structure likely to deliver clear, unambiguous decision-making. Decisions were taken and then rescinded at the next meeting, and debts mounted. Money was not available for other priorities, including flood prevention, with many parts of central Bath prone to frequent river flooding. So while Bath continued to be a popular resort for the leisured classes, it also continued to be a distressing and unhealthy home for those of the labouring classes. Yet, for all that, the Corporation continued to reign supreme, if not unchallenged, until the 1830s when the 1832 Reform Act and the 1835

RULERS AND RULED

Municipal Corporations Act finally put paid to the old oligarchic ways of ruling the city and representing its interests in parliament.

Polite Society and Radical Bath

If the Corporation exerted a firm grip on the economic life of the city, other forces were at work attempting to regulate the social life of the city. Richard "Beau" Nash arrived in Bath in 1705 at the age of thirty. Bath was disorganized and great fun, but open to all sorts of petty crime (including the activity of quack doctors) and licentious behaviour. Outside the baths and walking, there was little organized social activity. Master of Ceremonies in the city for much of the first half of the eighteenth century, Beau Nash introduced various improvements including a tariff for lodgings, street lighting provided by citizens, the filling of pot-holes, street-cleaning by citizens and controls on chairmen. He banned the wearing of swords and duels—both measures designed to take the sting out of gambling-fuelled quarrels. On the cultural front, he brought orchestras from London to play in Bath and encouraged the private chapels which became in turn centres of musical excellence. Many of these reforms were of a practical nature, but others related to a major problem in which Nash himself was implicated. How could gambling continue to be a major form of entertainment, and a major source of profit to Nash himself, without spilling over to violence in the streets which would discourage other visitors to the city? Gambling was a day-long activity that appealed both to men and women, and although banned in public rooms from 1745, private gambling continued.

It was also important to deal with snobbishness, both the reluctance of the nobles to have dealings with their "country cousins" and of the latter to have social dealings with tradesmen. Oliver Goldsmith put it like this:

> General society among people of rank and fashion was by no means established. The nobility still preserved a structure of Gothic haughtiness, and refused to keep company with the gentry at any of the public entertainments of the place. But when proper walks were made for exercise and a house built for assembling in, rank began to be laid

aside, and all degrees of people from the private gentleman upwards, were soon united with one another.

Bath was a polite society, with rules of etiquette and dress, and it was Nash who drew up the rules. Yet the phrase "from the private gentleman upwards", as Mark Girouard reminds us, was seriously meant. It was a democracy based on the possession of wealth. It was perfectly possible to be a member of the Corporation and not be able to meet the requirements to mix in the polite society of Bath. Civic dignitaries were not necessarily the sort of people that aristocratic visitors would want to meet on their evenings in the ballroom or at the card-tables. When modern commentators ask "Who is Bath for, residents or visitors?" they are asking a question which exercised their Georgian predecessors. Nash increased the business of the city by inducing an element of social levelling. As we shall see in Chapter 5, this social mixing in Bath was a subject for satire and mockery, but it did work. Contemporary commentators pointed out the irony that people would not acknowledge one another in London despite having been friends in Bath.

Nash may have been responsible for the social life of Bath's posh set, but it was the Corporation that had the very different responsibility for enforcing law and order in the city. Much crime was simply a by-product of poverty, a natural result of life in the teeming slums of Avon Street, where as many as 10,000 people (one-fifth of the population) lived in close and insanitary conditions. There were outbreaks of cholera in 1832 and of smallpox in 1839. But there was also a more threatening branch of criminality, one that went by the name of politics. In the 1790s England was a land divided between supporters and opponents of the French Revolution. In 1782 the awkwardly named Bath Association for Preserving Liberty, Property and the Constitution of Great Britain against Republicans and Levellers was established. We have already seen how the powerful could use the mob to their own ends, as in the burning of Tom Paine in effigy at Beechen Cliff in 1792. Even Hannah More, no friend of revolution, objected to the "drunken excesses of the Paine burning". In the words of historian Steve Poole, it was a Reign of Terror.

Benjamin Bull was arrested in 1794 for possession of a copy of Paine's book. He was sentenced to twelve months in prison and a twenty-shilling [one pound] fine, leaving his wife and five children destitute.

As Poole writes, our knowledge of radical working-class organizations at this time is sketchy, but certainly there was agitation, particularly at the turn of the century when bad harvests led to increased food prices and hunger. There is better evidence for more "respectable reformers" in two organizations established in 1792 and 1793. These were the Bath Society to Promote a Reform of Parliament and a More Equal Representation of the People, and the Bath Constitutional Society. By 1812 pressure was building for a more democratic way of electing Bath's MPs than the vote of thirty members of the Corporation. It was the freemen of the city, men of substance excluded from the Corporation, who led the charge. The 1812 election was pivotal in discrediting the old way of electing MPs, and in focusing popular discontent on electoral reform as well as more pressing issues such as food prices. For one of the very few times in recorded history, there was joint action with the radicals of Bristol, with petitions signed and large, noisy meetings held. The rejection of the first Reform Bill by the House of Lords in 1831 led to serious rioting in Bristol, with many buildings burned. The Bath troop of the North Somerset Yeomanry was despatched to Bristol to help control the mob, and for a while the workers of Bath controlled the streets. This led in turn to a meeting of 3000 men at the Tennis Court in Morford Street (now the Museum of Bath at Work) to form a Bath Political Union, controlled by the city's artisans. Following the passing of the 1832 Reform Act, at the first (partially) democratic election in Bath, with an electorate expanded from 30 to 3,000, the city elected an out-and-out radical John Roebuck alongside the long-time reformer and MP under the old system General Palmer.

Bath continued to be a stronghold of radical politics through the 1830s and 1840s, with the Chartists in the lead, populists who argued for an even wider extension of the franchise. Roebuck's programme of reform included universal suffrage (votes for all), a secret ballot, equal distribution of members in constituencies of similar size and shorter parliaments. In 1841 the *Bath Chronicle*, ever the supporter of conservative causes, expounded:

> Bath is a dark blot on the present general election. At a time when other places are, to their high honour, throwing off the trammels of modern Liberalism, Bath has put them on in their worst shape. It has returned not merely radicals or ultra-radicals, but persons who are "something more". We are taunted throughout the country with having sent to Parliament two disciples of revolution... "Hotbed of all that is wild, reckless, and revolutionary in politics" is the phrase which is abundantly used in speaking or writing of Bath.

It seems a very long time ago...

Victorian Preoccupations

From 1850 little was heard of radicalism in Bath. As the century progressed, the working class showed increasing support for the Liberal Party, which was seen as the party of non-conformity as well as temperance, an important movement in Bath. The only political position of the Trades and Labour Council, formed by the trade unions in 1891, was to urge support for Liberal candidates. In local government Bath adopted the gospel of public service, with social peace achieved by an increasing emphasis on municipal enterprise, whether in the form of street improvements, safe water supply or the city laundry next to the Roman Baths. It was personified in Jerom Murch, a Unitarian minister who settled in Bath in 1833 as Minister of Trim Street chapel. He was president of the Bath Literary and Philosophical Society for thirty years, a councillor from 1861, mayor seven times. It was his bequest which led to the founding of the City Art Gallery. At the 1851 religious census, religious attendance in Bath was second only to Hastings. The city remained one where the wealthy and privileged could go about their business without fear of the ambitions and hardships of the working classes.

For men at least (but certainly not for women) service trades were in decline. More of the men worked in the expanding industries of the city, with building accounting for no less than 16 per cent of male labour by 1901, as the city expanded into the suburbs far beyond its medieval and Georgian limits. But for women in 1901 domestic service remained the largest single category of employment (17 per cent of all women's jobs). The labour market remained rigidly divided with, for example, 325 female nurses and midwives, but only one woman doctor.

The Royal Victoria Park sums up many of the preoccupations of Victorian Bath. Previous to 1829 attempts had been made to build villas and cottages on the commons. The commons had long been a source of friction between Corporation and the freemen of the city, who were entitled to a share of the income from the land but not a share of political power. John Allen, the "people's choice" in the disputed election of 1812, was a freeman but not a member of the Corporation. The establishment of the park in 1829 preceded both the 1832 Reform Act and the 1835 Municipalities Act; it was run as a private organization and was not taken over by the Corporation until 1921. The Park Committee allowed the central commons (within the circular driveway) to continue to be used for grazing cattle, and the decorative *cottage orné* known as the Park Dairy can still be seen close to the obelisk dedicated to Queen Victoria. The park was the first Victoria Park in the country, since Victoria was a girl only eleven years old in 1829. The obelisk celebrated her eighteenth birthday and her accession to the throne in 1837.

It was originally intended that the Upper Common (on the hillside north of the Weston Road) would be part of the park, but this was never agreed, and this area is now a municipal golf course. The Lower Common, bordering on to the Upper Bristol Road, is now used for allotments, including a section run on organic lines under the aegis of the Bath Organic Group. (Yes, that does spell BOG.) Further west, the tiny children's playground in which I learned to love swings and hate roundabouts is now one of the largest of its kind in the country. A further group of allotments lie in the northeast corner of the park, between the back of Marlborough Buildings and the Weston Road. During and after the Second World War, the open land in front of the Royal Crescent was also used as allotments, but now is the preferred spot for open-air concerts, such as the Three Tenors concerts in anticipation of the opening of the new Bath Spa. There are also ponds on the Middle Common (there used to be a small boating pond) and the Botanical Gardens.

At one level, the opening up of the Victoria Park, bordering as it does on the high value Georgian areas of Queen Square, the Circus and the Royal Crescent, was intended to boost tourist numbers amid concern that many houses and shops were empty. Increasingly, though, it came to be understood as a leisure facility for the growing fixed population of the city, as well as the setting for the Georgian splendours of the Royal Crescent, a role it continues to play in the new Bath of international tourism.

Another major development in Bath during the nineteenth century was the growth of public education. In general, education was carefully controlled by the Church of England. After the school board was set up in 1871 it was controlled by the Anglicans until the end of the nineteenth century. Some new schools were created, but most remained in the hands of the Church. The non-conformist voice on the school board was important, however, since two women (a Quaker and a Wesleyan Methodist) were elected, the first time that the male domination of power in the city had been challenged. School boards were not popular with the more conservative elements in Bath, and the *Bath Chronicle* in 1896 referred to "piling up the rates", a criticism often used to refer to municipal initiatives which the wealthy would never use. Twerton had a separate school board and three new schools were established to complement the existing church school. But progress was slow, with the Vicar of Twerton chairing the board protecting the Church of England interest and Jonathan Carr of Carr's Mill, the largest Twerton employer, making sure that no extravagant expenditure was incurred. It was to be the late 1880s before sufficient school places were available for all the children in Twerton.

While both Bath and Twerton moved cautiously to establish a system of elementary schools, it was to be well into the twentieth century before they established secondary education. It took some years for even elementary schooling to be accepted as part of the normal fabric of working-class life. In his history of public education in Bath, *Unwillingly to School*, Horace Brand, Director of Education from the 1950s to 1970, refers to the many problems to be overcome in setting up a system of public education. In addition to the fees charged initially, other difficulties encountered included poverty leading to malnutrition and genuine ill-health and truanting because of children needing to supplement parental income. It was an uphill task.

Decline and Revival

As we move into the twentieth century, the story of "rulers and ruled" in Bath becomes increasingly part of national history. Local ties were loosened, with people moving into Bath from other towns and rural areas, and Bath men and women also becoming more mobile. The inter-war years were perhaps the low point of Bath as a special place, England's premier spa. The Assembly Rooms were redundant and closed in 1921, with the ballroom turned into a cinema, catering to the new mass entertainment. Like other spa towns, Bath continued to decline at the expense of seaside resorts. It had become a drab city, its buildings blackened by constant exposure to soot from chimneys and steam locomotives. Many of the fine Georgian houses were subdivided at this period into flats and offices—of course many had been built originally as apartment houses—while new building continued in the suburbs. Of just over 4000 new houses built, about 1000 were council houses. It was short of the "homes fit for heroes" the returning soldiers had been promised, but it was a start at least. There were rumours of council contracts going to "insiders"—councillors and aldermen who were also local building contractors, an accusation that resurfaced again when the urgent task of rebuilding after the Second World War Bath blitz arose.

Unemployment was high, reaching 3000 (about ten per cent) in 1932, but the local economy remained fairly buoyant. By 1937 Bath was attracting workers from South Wales and the North of England. Projects such as the restoration of the Assembly Rooms, which was completed in 1938, and the fine new secondary school for boys on Beechen Cliff created jobs. Yet poor housing and poverty contributed to high levels of tuberculosis, reckoned at thirteen per cent of all schoolchildren in the early 1930s.

Of importance to the future of Bath as a World Heritage Site were the Local Acts of 1925 and 1937. These did not save the so-called "minor" Georgian buildings from the Sack of Bath, but did offer some protection again insensitive modernization of the more distinguished survivors. The Bath blitz was a major disaster; the reality of the Baedeker raids of April 1942 was 400 killed, nearly one thousand injured and 2600 uninjured but bombed out of their houses. My parents' home was damaged sufficiently for them to have to move out to temporary accommodation, where my elder sister was born, while it was repaired. The mass graves at Haycombe Cemetery on the hillside overlooking Englishcombe are carefully maintained and another reminder of the horror of war. One of the most momentous aspects of the Second World War was the arrival of the Admiralty in Bath, and its decision to stay put after the war, quickly becoming a major employer in the city. In many ways this re-introduced Bath into a wider world beyond its surrounding hills. Other symptoms of modernization in the city included the rapidly expanding council housing estates and the building of new schools in the immediate post-war period.

Yet socially and politically Bath retained a rather conservative feel about it. It still attracted those looking for a retirement home with more social pretensions than ready cash. The City Council had inherited much of the old Corporation's property portfolio, plus ownership of major attractions such as the Pump Room and Roman Baths. In the early 1980s this was reckoned to be worth nine pence in the pound off the local taxes. Old and new Bath clashed repeatedly over the issue of what kind of city it wanted to be. Often it was outsiders to the city who led the opposition to proposals to change its appearance, as in the demolition of Georgian houses north of the London Road at Snow Hill and their replacement by Bath's first and (to date) only high-rise building. The Abercrombie Plan of 1945, which would have seen the Royal Crescent transformed into a new civic centre, was rejected. Later, the protracted arguments about Colin Buchanan's report on traffic in the city, and his proposal for an

RULERS AND RULED

east-west tunnel under the city centre was the catalyst for a growing number of organizations opposed to change: Bath Action Group, Bath Environmental Campaign, Bath Amenity and Transport Association and Save Bath. It is hard to know what the average Bath resident made of these debates, and yet their outcome has impacted on everyone who lives there.

All cities have a tendency to grow, but Bath is a static city, and must be so in order to protect its heritage, its skyline and the environmentally sensitive area in which it lies. In a market economy this means that property prices rise. With the cessation of new council house building and the selling off of many of the best quality houses from 1980, many children of Bath families have been forced to look elsewhere for housing, especially to the towns and villages of the old coalfield on the northern slopes of the Mendips. This has strengthened the newcomer element to the city, and newcomers now dominate many of its local organizations and its local government. The designation of Bath as a Unesco World Heritage Site in 1987 has offered only a provisional answer to the question "Who is Bath for?" Bath is for the visitor and those lucky or rich enough to be able to live there. The one thing these influential newcomers to the city have been unable to prevent is the creation of new local government structures that reflect the relative wealth of the city and the relative poverty, and in some cases high levels of social need, in other surrounding areas. Avon County (1974-96) was not a success. Cautious Bath and dynamic Bristol just do not mix. Bath and North East Somerset, which slots Bath in with precisely those places where "Bath people" have sought refuge in recent years, is rather more successful. Yet if we return again to politics, there has at last been change, with the election of a Liberal Democrat MP in 1992 and at all elections since. Bath may be firmly within the grasp of the middle classes, but they are a younger, more cosmopolitan, more outward-looking bunch than those who dominated Bath politics for more than a century from the 1850s.

Which brings us neatly back to the present day. Bath is not an easy city to govern: a static city with a mobile population; a city proud of its local roots but always conscious of its World Heritage status; a cramped city hemmed in by hills and overrun by road traffic. Local politicians and officers do their best, but at times it is hard going. The Buchanan saga and the consequent planning blight dragged on for years. Then there was the Batheaston bypass saga where protesters, some of whom built homes high up in the trees on the route of the new road, fiercely opposed plans to build a link road across the meadows from the A46 to the A36 roads. That ended with a scar on the landscape that fails completely to achieve the original objective to create a north-south link bypassing Bath. As for the "redevelopment" of the friendly, messy Southgate Street I knew as a child in the late 1960s and early 1970s, Bath builder and developer Cyril Beazer described it in these terms: "The demolition and rebuilding of Southgate Street can only be described as the height of folly, verging on scandal." This was a project so bad that a second redevelopment had to be undertaken in the twenty-first century. The issues and scandals multiply.

The failure of the city authorities to secure the Dyson Academy of Engineering Design in the early years of this century is instructive. Initially Dyson was promised the Newark Works of Stothert & Pitt in Lower Bristol Road, across the river from the City of Bath College (the Tech). The conservation lobby then discovered this was an early work by a local architect who subsequently became famous as the architect of the Canadian Parliament in Ottawa. Cue total revision of plans, retaining the façade and developing a new building behind it. Then the Environment Agency raised the old issue of flooding to which the Newark Works had been very prone. Dyson lost patience and abandoned his plans, though exactly what the mixture was in his decision-making between the pusillanimity of local politicians, the cautious central government and its officials and his own sense of the oncoming financial crisis and recession beginning in 2008, we shall probably never know. Projects in Bath are big, the risks enormous. The spa project came in late and vastly over-budget. It also trailed a series of legal cases which have, thankfully, been settled out-of-court, to the chagrin of lawyers no doubt but to the satisfaction of the local authority, which will have one less set of expenses to meet.

Then there is the Western Riverside, the large area west of Green Park station which was once the home of the Somerset and Dorset Railway and of Stothert & Pitt. What sort of mix of housing and business and retail and cultural uses might be appropriate here? What kind of public transport requirements might there be to get the new residents of this new zone of the city to and fro? Could there be a new home here for Bath Rugby (see Chapter 7), who continue to occupy the Recreation Ground despite the contradictions with its charitable status as a recreational facility for all Bathonians and all sports? In 2009 Jonathan Glancey, architectural correspondent of *The Guardian*, entered the fray with an article headlined "Bath Keeps its World Heritage Status—Just". One of Unesco's complaints was the poor design quality of the proposed new housing crammed on to the Western Riverside site. And to that might be added the caution of local planners who have failed even to attempt to meet Bath's need for an international concert hall to house its international music festival.

The Wife of Bath

The Written Word
Bath in Literature

"Allas, allas, that evere love was sinne!"
Geoffrey Chaucer, The Wife of Bath's Tale

In the Beginning was Chaucer

Apart from a fragment of Anglo-Saxon poetry grieving at the mighty city brought low by abandon and neglect, it is Chaucer, the Father of English Poetry, who first brings Bath to the attention of a reading public. The Wife of Bath is an extraordinary literary creation—opinionated, amusing, rude, full of a kind of rough wisdom. Her scarlet stockings and gap teeth both suggest a woman with a voracious sexual appetite, as do her five husbands and her youthful "wandrynge by the weye". She is well travelled, having been to Rome three times, to the shrine of St. James at Santiago de Compostela in Galicia, as well as having made more modest trips within England and the near continent. She is also rooted in the economy of medieval England. She is a cloth-maker who can compete with the best weavers of Flanders—Ypres and Ghent are both mentioned by name.

Chaucer is pleased with his Wife of Bath. In the prologue to the tale she will tell he allows her to embroider further the portrait offered in the General Prologue, in particular her views on marriage, based on her own extensive experience. The tale she tells then exhibits her view that women must have the upper hand in marriage (her main argument is the rather less than feminist one that otherwise they will create merry hell and make their husbands' lives a misery).

Perhaps because of her rather controversial views on love and marriage, the Wife of Bath has been largely ignored by later centuries of Bathonians. No statue, no street. Chaucer does give his name to one of the Edwardian terraces climbing the south side of Beechen Cliff, but only alongside more respectable English literary figures: Shakespeare, Milton, Kipling, Longfellow and Shelley. There is no equivalent of Coventry's Lady Godiva clock, for example, despite the obvious visual qualities to the portrait given by Chaucer. Women, as both writers and characters, have loomed large in the literary life of Bath. Yet only Jane Austen, it seems, has ever received a high approval rating in the city—which is odd, as we shall see.

Travellers' Tales and Satirists' Stories

Given the fame of Georgian and Regency Bath, it is unsurprising that most of the writers mentioned in this chapter are from that period in the city's history, when just about everybody of note passed through. But already in the seventeenth century Bath was acquiring considerable fame, and was an essential stopover for any writer with ambitions to give a broad view of English society. Samuel Pepys the diarist passed this way in 1668. Having got up at 4 o'clock in the morning to avoid the crush at the Cross Bath, he was not altogether convinced of the merits of communal bathing, though the questionable propriety of it seems to have caused him no bother. He wrote:

> And by and by though we designed to have done before company came, much company came, very fine ladies and the manner pretty enough, only methinks it cannot be clean to go so many bodies together in to the same water. Good conversation among them that are acquainted here and stay together. Strange to see how hot the water is and in some places though this is the most temperate bath the springs so hot as the feet not to endure. But strange to see what women and men herein that live all the season in these waters that cannot but be parboiled and look like creatures of the Bath. Carried back wrapped in a sheet and in a chair home…

Strange to think when soaking in the Cross Bath 250 years later (though certainly not at 4 o'clock in the morning) that we are wallowing in the same hot spring where Samuel Pepys once lay. Another seventeenth-century visitor was the indefatigable Celia Fiennes, a lady of strong opinions though uncertain spelling and punctuation, which only add to the rigour of her opinions. In the following extract, which probably refers to the year 1687, she comments that the water was already being used for drinking as well as bathing, and on the relative lack of organized amusements in the city:

> Ye Queens bath is a degree hotter than ye Cross bath and ye Kings bath much hotter, these have all galleryes round and the pump is in one of these gallery's at ye Kings bath which ye Company drinks of, it is very hot and tastes like the water that boyles Eggs, has such a smell, but ye nearer the pumpe you drink it, ye hotter and less offencive and more spirituous.
>
> Ye places for divertion about ye bath is either ye walkes in that they call ye Kings Mead which is a pleasant green meadow, where are walkes round and Cross it, no place for Coaches...

Jonathan Swift, in his *Tour through the Whole Island of Britain*, published in the 1720s, finds it hard to keep a straight face about Bath. He is less impressed by Bath and its spa waters than he is by nearby Frome and its industrious weavers, for example. Having given a perfunctory nod in the direction of King Bladud, he continues:

> There remains little to add, but what relates to the Modern Customs, the Gallantry and Diversions of that Place, in which I shall be very short; the best part being but a Barren Subject, and the worst Part meriting rather a Satyr, than a description.

The praise is so faint it is scarcely perceptible.

It was Beau Nash as Master of Ceremonies who attempted successfully to remedy the lack of organized social activities, and to set rules for the conduct of polite social life (Celia Fiennes' "Company") in Bath. Oliver Goldsmith, in his life of Nash, published in 1762, paid a generous tribute to the great man, though even he could not avoid a certain element of gentle mockery:

> We are now to behold this gentleman as arrived at a new dignity for which nature seemed to have formed him; we are to see him directing pleasures, which none had better learned to share; placed over rebellious and refractory subjects that were to be ruled only by the force of his address, and governing such as had been long accustomed to govern others. We see a kingdom beginning with him and sending off Tunbridge [Tunbridge Wells in Kent] as one of its colonies.

By the time Tobias Smollett came to write *Humphrey Clinker* (1771), which has a substantial section set in Bath, a new Master of Ceremonies was in place. This is an epistolary novel, a form that allows different characters in their letters to set up competing views of the city. While Matthew Bramble, the central character, pours scorn on the Master of Ceremonies as a servile, self-seeking fop, Lydia Melford sees him as a charming, courteous man eager to smooth the absorption of new arrivals into the social whirl of Bath:

> As soon as we were settled into lodgings, we were visited by the Master of Ceremonies; a pretty little gentleman, so sweet, so fine, so civil and polite, that in our country he might pass for the prince of Wales; then he talks so charmingly, both in verse and prose, that you would be delighted to hear him discourse; for you must know he is a great writer.

Most of Smollett's readers would have known that the man described was Samuel Derrick, a notorious hack writer and contributor to Smollett's *Critical Review*.

Another writer with a keen eye and ear for the funny side of Bath life was the dramatist Richard Brinsley Sheridan. Sheridan is an enigma. He wrote two of the most popular comedies in the English stage repertoire (*The Rivals*, set in Bath, and the wildly satirical *School for Scandal*) and was owner of the Drury Lane Theatre in London's Covent Garden. But was his heart really in the theatre? His elopement with the young singer Elizabeth Linley, on whose behalf he fought two duels, was one of the great scandals of eighteenth-century Bath. He became a Member of Parliament and a government minister, but was plagued throughout his life by financial troubles (a spendthrift rather than a gambler). His theatre was burned to the ground in 1809, he lost his parliamentary seat in 1811, and was arrested for debt in 1813. He died in 1816. He had hoped to be buried next to his political mentor Charles James Fox. Instead he was laid to rest next to the actor and producer David Garrick, a man whose name is still remembered at the Garrick's Head, the pub next door to Bath's Theatre Royal.

Dictates of Fashion

The transformation of Bath from a rather seedy seventeenth-century town to the fashionable Georgian city had been largely accomplished by the mid-century. John Wood had set the style in architecture, Beau Nash in social mores. It had been done with royal approval, too. When Queen Elizabeth visited Bath, a major royal concern had been to upbraid the citizens about the ruinous state of the abbey church. When Anne of Denmark, wife of James I visited to bathe in the waters in 1616, this must have raised a few eyebrows at court. We have already noted that James II's wife, Mary of Modena, a devout Catholic, was widely believed to have conceived following a visit to take the spa waters in Bath. Queen Anne visited Bath in 1702 and enjoyed herself so much that she came back the following year. The Corporation was (at least in eighteenth-century terms) progressive and forward-looking, Beau Nash and John Wood came on board, Ralph Allen was organizing his Bath stone quarries into a major industry. Bath was afloat on a sea of fashion, gambling, gossip and intrigue. What better place for a writer to be!

As Christopher Anstey noted in his *New Bath Guide* (1766), the gently satirical tone of which was to influence both Smollett and (two centuries later) John Betjeman:

> Let Bristol for commerce and dirt be renown'd,
> At Sal'sbury pen-knives and scissors be ground;
> The towns of Devizes, of Bradford and Frome,
> May boast that they better can manage the loom;
> I believe that they may; - but the world to refine,

THE WRITTEN WORD

In manners, in dress, in politeness to shine,
O Bath! - let the art, let the glory be thine.

The glory—and the cash too. Oliver Goldsmith, apart from his major role in writing up the reputation of Beau Nash and not writing up the list of young men who lost heavily at his gaming tables, gives a detailed account of how the social life in Bath was developing from the initial activity of taking the waters, now confined to the early hours of the morning. Visitors would gather at the Pump Room to drink the waters—now considered as health-giving as bathing in them—and indulge in gossip to the strains of a little light music. The little light music is still a feature of daytime visits to the Pump Room, though most visitors find the waters, warm and strong, not to their taste. From the Pump Room, men and women went in different directions, the women to their lodgings for breakfast or to women-only coffee houses, the men to their own coffee-houses to read the newspapers or discuss the news. More fashionable visitors might invite their friends to attend musical breakfasts in the Assembly Rooms. Later in the day, shopping, walks, rides in carriages or on horseback would be the main activities, while in the evening there were plays, card parties, dances and balls at the Assembly Rooms. Bath, concluded Goldsmith, "yields a continued rotation of diversions, and people of all ways of thinking, even from the libertine to the Methodist, have it in their power to complete the day with employments suited to their inclinations." Goldsmith would without doubt have done well on the travel pages of a modern Sunday paper. Jane Austen, as we shall see, was a rather more cautious and nuanced supporter of the city.

Smollett's Lydia Melford remarks that "Bath is to me a new world - All is gayety, good-humour, and diversion." But it is Bramble who steals the show and most clearly reflects the author's own point of view with his sardonic reflections on the visitors, the customs of the place, the grand designs of John Wood, the inflated prices and the "madness of the times":

Bath is become a mere sink of profligacy and extortion. Every article of housekeeping is raised to an enormous price; a circumstance no longer to be wondered at, when we know that every petty retainer of fortunes piques himself upon keeping a table, and thinks 'tis for the honour of his character to wink at the knavery of his servants, who are in a confederacy with the market people; and, of consequence, pay whatever they demand.

It is a grave error to view Georgian Bath as a single entity. As we shall see in Chapter 8 when we consider religion, from mid-century there are noticeable changes in Bath, with an increasingly moralistic tone and a greater emphasis on organized religion, both of the traditional Anglican variety and also the various non-conformist sects, noticeably the Methodists. In some ways, this was also a division between male and female views of the city and of the wider society. But since we have begun with the men, we may as well continue with them, especially as a consideration of women writers in Georgian Bath will run seamlessly into some thoughts on Jane Austen whose stays in Bath bring us right to the end of the eighteenth century.

There was no clear distinction in the first half of the century between popular fiction and what we might now call soft pornography. James Leake, the city's main printer and bookseller, published his notorious *A New Description of Merryland*, with the author masquerading as one Roger Phfuquewell, while Merryland was nothing less than a thinly disguised woman's body. Needless to say, the book sold well. Although we shall not pause long over Leake's brother-in-law, Samuel Richardson, it is helpful to observe that the rivalry between Richardson and Henry Fielding was not so much about which wrote the steamier, sexier, more suggestive stories, but about how this might be dressed up as somehow a "moral tale". The very subtitle of Richardson's first novel, *Pamela: Or Virtue Rewarded* (1740), suggests such a moral intent, while the heroine of his *Clarissa* is killed off after nearly a million words to make the point that happiness is to be expected in the next world rather than this. He was as adept at bodice-ripping sex-and-violence as Fielding, but the author of *Tom Jones* adopts a more amoral approach to his stories.

Henry Fielding

Fielding is Bath's best-known novelist after Austen. Born at Sharpham Park, near Glastonbury, and raised near Mere in Dorset, he saw the proper ordering of landscape, ideally as part of a gentleman's park, as having moral value. He wrote *Tom Jones* in Twerton, a fact that now seems implausible, since Twerton is the other side of Bath: working-class, industrial, grimy. Yet in Fielding's day Brunel's grim Great Western Railway viaduct that strides straight through this part of Bath glancing neither to left nor right was still nearly a hundred years away. There were pleasant water-meadows, and fields stretching up to the high scarp of the Cotswolds at Lansdown. His house on the north side of the Lower Bristol Road, a little towards the city from the Golden Fleece pub, was demolished early in the twentieth century to make way for industrial buildings. Now student housing occupies the site. And when he was not sitting in Twerton writing and mourning his wife Charlotte, immortalized as the sweet Sophia Western of the novel, he was living the good life up at Prior Park with his friends Ralph Allen and Alexander Pope, sometimes even his novelist sister Sarah Fielding, despite her preference for the distinctly more respectable Richardson.

Is Squire Allworthy in *Tom Jones* to be identified with Ralph Allen? Firstly and quite clearly, Henry Fielding wanted to please his open-handed patron, and Allworthy is both good-hearted and generous. Fielding writes that "Neither Mr Allworthy's house nor his heart were shut against any part of mankind, but they were both more particularly open to men of merit. To say the truth, this was the only house in the kingdom where you were sure to gain a good dinner by deserving it." No doubt Fielding was sure that he deserved the many good dinners he had at Allen's expense. Yet of course Allen was a businessman, an entrepreneur, a capitalist, rather than a country squire. He had made a fortune out of reforming the postal trade between Bath and London, and invested much of the money in acquiring the stone quarries on Combe Down, financing improvements in the river navigation between Bristol and Bath to reduce transport costs and building a tramway down what is Ralph Allen Drive to carry stone to the riverside. Prior Park was an advertisement for the virtues and properties of Bath stone, and much of the time Allen preferred his town house just south of Bath Abbey with its fine view up the slopes to Sham Castle, another of his creations, or his manor house on the meadows at Bathampton, just to the east of the city.

Women Writers

Now for the women. Sarah Fielding, sister of Henry, was a kept woman. Not in the modern sense, but certainly she was financially dependent. Henry was simply hopeless with money, and Sarah, like her brother, depended greatly on the patronage of Ralph Allen, which enabled her to live comfortably at Widcombe Lodge, close to the manor and the church. She settled in Bath from 1758 and in addition to the house received an annuity of one hundred pounds from Ralph Allen. Before her death she was discussing with the well-known bluestocking Elizabeth Montagu and her sister Sarah Scott plans to set up a community of women along the lines of Scott's novel *A Description of Millennium Hall*. Sarah Fielding published a successful novel *David Simple* which revealed her knowledge of suffering (her three sisters all died in a seven-month period in 1750/1), her advanced social ideas and her strict morality. Her 1749 novel *The Governess* has been described as "the first fictional story written especially for young people". It was her stern view that literature must have a moral purpose, a view shared (however cynically) by Richardson, and one can only imagine how hard she must have found it not to disapprove of her dissolute brother and his novels. Sarah Fielding was buried at Charlcombe Church, where her brother had been married; there is also a memorial in Bath Abbey which praises her writings "as Incentives to Virtue and an Honour to her Sex".

Sarah Scott initially went to Bath for her health, but soon moved in with Barbara Montagu, usually referred to in bluestocking circles as Lady Bab, perhaps to distinguish her from Elizabeth Montagu, Sarah's sister and no relation of Barbara. There was gossip, but no evidence either for or against the claim that they were a lesbian couple. Her first novel was published in 1750 and her work fits very closely within a bluestocking framework—the attempt to reform fashionable society, eliminate drinking and gambling and to create what her modern editor Gary Kelly describes as "a space for women's intellectual life and a centre for women's Christian patronage and philanthropy". It fitted too, and indeed contributed towards, the changing emphasis in Bath from the mid-century onwards. Sarah acquired her surname by marriage to George Scott in 1751, a marriage probably never consummated. It failed and Sarah returned to Bath to a life of writing and good works, shared with Lady Bab and the Bath bluestockings, centred on the village of Batheaston, but through her sister Elizabeth she was also linked closely into the wider London-centred bluestocking world.

Despite her literary and political conservatism, Scott's *A Description of Millennium Hall* (1762), her most reprinted book, is socially very advanced with its feminized version of country estate life revolving around a group of women seen as victims of the "courtly, patriarchal and mercenary society" (Kelly again) beyond Millennium Hall. There are themes here that twentieth-century feminism would take up with vigour: the possibilities of women-only communities, the struggle for economic and social independence from men, the need to reform manners and behaviour. Yet the tone is dramatically different, with the eighteenth-century emphasis on social distance, the notion that the lower classes should know their place and stay there, the assumption that upper-class women must always know better.

There were contradictions in the bluestocking view of the world, and nowhere do they emerge as sharply as in the work of Hannah More, another writer very closely connected with Bath. We are indebted to Norma Clarke in her book *Dr Johnson's Women* for the most clear-sighted account of the struggle of literary women in eighteenth-century England. Dr. Johnson was the patron-in-chief, easing the path of his chosen *protégées* to publication and a level of independence they would otherwise have struggled to achieve. In addition to Johnson's support, the young Hannah More also received assistance from David and Eva Garrick. As a young woman, Hannah and her sisters ran a school for young ladies in Bristol, a school attended by various daughters of the Theatre Royal Bristol Company. Hannah became involved with the theatrical world of Bristol and Bath, and her play *The Inflexible Captive* was put on in Bath in 1775. David Garrick himself wrote the epilogue. *Percy* was an outstanding success and made money for both the Garricks and More: the great Sarah Siddons herself appeared in *Percy* when it was performed at Bath in 1778.

But More's interests were now reaching beyond the fashionable and often scandalous world of the theatre. Her moralizing became more severe, and at one point Eva Garrick was employing her as a household chaplain with responsibility for the moral and spiritual welfare of the servants. Religion and the abolition of the slave trade became her overriding concerns. "God almighty has set before me two great objects," she wrote, "the suppression of the slave trade and the reformation of manners." Norma Clarke insists on seeing More as a conservative figure:

> Hannah More's loyalties were with the established order and this may explain her viciousness towards the one woman of her time who represented the repudiation of deference culture, who dedicated her books to the leaders of the French Revolution, and who claimed rights for women: Mary Wollstonecraft.

This is not entirely fair. More set up a network of schools in villages in North Somerset and despite their very orthodox curriculum, there were controversies. More than once she was accused of Methodism by establishment figures for whom any attempt to bring education to the labouring classes was anathema. A similar point might be made about the bluestockings in general. Sarah Scott lived in Norwich in the 1790s, a Jacobin centre, and shared with Edmund Burke feelings of horror and revulsion at the French Revolution. Yet just as More found herself smeared with Methodism, which Scott described as "a dangerous form of plebeian presumption", for her schools, so Scott and the bluestockings found themselves smeared with Jacobinism for criticizing a society in which the cards were stacked firmly on the side of men. The scene was set for the Victorian

Age and a further tightening of the already circumscribed lives of young women.

The novelist and diarist Fanny Burney (1752-1840) was another *protégée* of the ubiquitous Dr. Johnson, of whom she left an engaging portrait in her posthumously published diaries. Indeed, some critics prefer her account of Johnson's character and doings to the better known diaries of Boswell. The three novels for which she is remembered—*Evelina, Cecilia* and *Camilla*—all portray beautiful but naive heroines learning to survive in the hurly-burly of eighteenth-century polite society, flitting between its London base and its pleasure grounds in Bath and other fashionable resorts. In 1793 Burney married a French émigré Alexandre d'Arblay, and in subsequent years spent considerable time in France. Despite her longevity, her health was never strong, and in 1811 she had a mastectomy without anaesthetic, of which she left a vivid account in her correspondence. Although she died in London, she is buried next to her son in St. Swithin's Walcot. Perhaps of all the women writers connected with Bath whose reputations have tended to decline with the years, it is Burney who is most due a revival, for her diaries and letters as much as for her novels.

One exception to the conservatism of clever women in eighteenth-century Bath is the historian Catharine Macaulay. She was painted in 1775 by the Bath artist Robert Edge Pine, a remarkable picture now in the National Portrait Gallery in London. Both Pine and Macaulay had strong republican sympathies, and she is portrayed in Roman dress with her right hand resting on the first five published volumes of her monumental *History of England*. The books rest on a plinth adorned with the words "GOVERNMENT – A POWER DELEGATED FOR THE HAPPINESS OF MANKIND". Macaulay was a supporter of John Wilkes, whose radical "Wilkes and Liberty" campaign enlivened English politics at the time, and of Cromwell's Commonwealth, which she described as "the brightest age that ever adorned the page of history". In her left hand Macaulay holds a letter addressed to a wealthy Church of England clergyman and widower, Thomas Wilson. Macaulay and Wilson caused a great scandal in Bath by sharing a house in Alfred

Street. Wilson was besotted with her, but Macaulay deepened the scandal by marrying in 1778 not Wilson, but William Graham, a ship surgeon's mate. She was 47 years old, he was 21.

Jane Austen

And what shall we say of Jane Austen? First we might mention that Mary Wollstonecraft had lived briefly in Bath as a young woman, as a lady's companion. While Austen was writing her first stories, Wollstonecraft was writing her *Vindication of the Rights of Women*, a text that shocked conservatives and liberals alike, but of which Macaulay approved. While Wollstonecraft stands close to the camera lens of history, Austen is a slightly out-of-focus figure in the middle distance, an enigma, and the careful destruction by family members of any letters that might help to unravel the enigma has not helped. She is not of course the only writer of the period with a decidedly limited view of what might constitute society. A similar criticism might be made of the bluestockings. Perhaps less so of the men— Fielding, Smollett, a little later Dickens—but as men they had easier access to the soft underbelly of society, the rogues and rascals, the thieves and cheats, the prostitutes and the kept women. The social world of Austen's novels is exactly what was available to Austen herself: a network of country houses, of fashionable spa towns. Other people did the real work of society, we might say. Just as Jane Austen loved walking to Weston, but makes no comment on its sturdy washerwomen, so she writes in her letters of the problem of flooding and general unhealthiness of the low-lying Green Park area, but fails to note its contiguity to the crowded slums of Avon Street. Hers is a world of private parties (increasingly beginning to replace the public assemblies and balls), churches judged on the quality of their fires rather than the fire in the belly of the preacher, fireworks in Sydney Garden, young women reading Gothic novels in the tradition of Horace Walpole's *The Castle of Otranto* and Anne Radcliffe's *The Mysteries of Udolpho* from bookshops and circulating libraries. None of this is to minimize the triumph of her novels, but to suggest their very partial view of eighteenth-century Bath. There is a sensibility in Austen, but it is turned inwards, a little world indeed.

The enigma of Jane Austen is eclipsed, in my own view, by the mysterious and exceptional cult of Jane Austen which exists in the city and the nation. Given that Bath is full of visitors, we must consider both in order to come to some conclusions about the matter. No-one disputes that Austen, within the limitations imposed by her own life and experience, was a good writer. Or that the straightforward stories she composed make good films and costume dramas for the cinema and television. But what is really surprising is that of all the forms of escapism available in the modern world, Jane Austen's cramped little world is felt to be so desirable. Bath has its Jane Austen Centre in Gay Street (between Queen Square and the Circus) and it is one of the city's most popular attractions. Each September there is a weeklong Jane Austen Festival. There are talks, films, drama productions, much as one might expect. But a key part of this annual celebration is the "Grand Regency costumed parade" (it used to be Georgian, but the world moves on) which attracts over 400 participants to parade (or is it stroll or saunter) through the streets of Bath dressed in their early nineteenth-century finery.

Turning briefly to Jane Austen's own writing, two novels have Bath settings—her first, *Northanger Abbey*, and her last, *Persuasion*, although in the event both were published together after her death in 1818. The first of these is a thinly disguised satire on the cult of the Gothic novel. Catherine Morland is a rather ordinary young woman, and it is through her excited, young eyes that we see the snobbish, rather pretentious world of Bath. Even landscape is seen as a kind of fashion accessory, the sort of landscape which Ralph Allen, initially inspired by Alexander Pope, had tried to create at Prior Park or the banking Hoares had established at Stourhead. On a walk, Henry Tilney lectures Catherine Morland on the "picturesque", such that "Catherine was so hopeful a scholar, that when they gained the top of Beechen Cliff, she voluntarily rejected the whole city of Bath, as unworthy to make part of a landscape." We know from her letters that this was a favourite view of Austen's and it is this tendency towards the satirical, the ironical, that made her such a vigorous and effective commentator on the social life of her class and times.

If Catherine Morland is young and impressionable, Anne Elliott in *Persuasion* is not quite young and rather jaundiced with life. Clearly she prefers the country to the city. From her arrival in Bath, the author makes it clear that her heroine "persisted in a very determined, though very silent, disinclination for Bath". All is well, eventually, and no doubt Anne and her beloved Captain Wentworth will live happily ever after. But it will not be in Bath. It is interesting to compare Austen's view with that of a contemporary visitor to Bath, Louis Simond, who in 1810 referred to it in these terms: "Bath is a sort of great monastery, inhabited by single people, particularly superannuated females. No trade, no manufacture, no occupations of any sort, except of killing time, the most laborious of all." Except, perhaps, for shopping: "Multitudes of splendid shops, full of all that wealth and luxury can desire, arranged with all the arts of seduction."

Thomas Beckford and Charles Dickens

Only one Bathonian disliked Bath more than Jane Austen, William Thomas Beckford. His views on Bath and on architecture can be found in Chapter 12, but here we mention and indeed honour his writing. Beckford (1760-1844) was the richest man in Europe, though his money did not come from Europe but from the slave plantations of Jamaica. He was formidably well read and equally well travelled. He studied Goethe in German; he was an Orientalist, well versed in Arab and Persian culture and history; he knew the bizarre flights of architectural fantasy in Piranesi's designs; he was the greatest collector of his time. His official 21st birthday party was followed by a four-day unofficial orgy, designed by Jacques Philippe de Loutherbourg. He claimed this party as the origin of many of the scenes in his novel *Vathek*, written in French in the early 1780s and published in English in 1786. *Vathek* is a footnote. It both drew on and helped to establish a fashion for exotic tales set in Arab countries, full of passion and lurid, macabre and sometimes sadistic adventures difficult to imagine in eighteenth-century Bath.

A reluctant resident of the city from 1823, Beckford lived as a recluse in Lansdown Crescent with his own private landscaped garden route up to the Lansdown Tower (later renamed after him), which he visited daily, riding up and walking down the steep slopes. In Bath he established himself as one of the great English art collectors and wrote too, revising some of his travel writings from the previous century, notably *Recollections of an Excursion to the Monasteries of Alcobaça and Batalha*. They fitted neatly into just that cult of the picturesque and sublime which Austen had poked fun at on Beechen Cliff, and were well received. But his final writings, the *Liber Veritatis*, the Book of Truth, are described by James Lee-Milne as "prickly, malign and embittered". They were not published until nearly one hundred years after his death.

After Austen, and still in Beckford's lifetime, comes Charles Dickens. His first great success, *Pickwick Papers*, was published in 1837, just twenty years after the death of Jane Austen. Chapters 35-39 are set in Bath, with a related episode in Bristol, about one-tenth of the whole. It is hard to believe that Dickens was unaware of Smollett and *Humphrey Clinker*. Dickens' Master of Ceremonies Angelo Cyrus Bantam is uncannily close to Smollett's own MC, while the use of bizarre names again recalls Smollett. Witness the following exchange:

> "Any body here?" inquired Dowler suspiciously.
> "Any body! The élite of Ba-ath. Mr Pickwick, do you see the lady in the gauze turban?"
> "The fat old lady?" inquired Mr Pickwick, innocently.
> "Hush, my dear Sir—nobody's fat or old in Ba-ath. That's the dowager Lady Snuphanuph."

No doubt all too many Bathonians of the period were both fat and old. Dickens is done with Bath quite quickly. *Pickwick Papers* required both action and characters to maintain its rollicking pace, and the main action takes place elsewhere. Dickens damns with faint praise the routine of the season in Bath—taking the waters, the Pump Room, the Assembly Rooms, the theatre—"a very pleasant routine, with perhaps a slight tinge of sameness".

Betjeman and Beyond

It is that "slight tinge of sameness" that was to cast a shadow over the cultural and social life of Bath for many years to come. Bath ceases to impinge on the literary life and imaginings of England, either as a place of residence or as raw material for literature. Until, that is, the arrival of John Betjeman as a civilian intelligence officer attached to the Admiralty. For Betjeman, Bath was traditional England, real architecture, the comfortable life of the middle classes with their genteel amusements and pastimes—tea-drinking, crochet, croquet, and a little adultery on the side. It has taken the critics some time to work out that "such an ordinary little woman" in the poem "In a Bath Tea-shop" is not some woman that the misogynistic poet was observing having tea but a married woman with whom the same poet was carrying on an affair. And there were others too as Betjeman's marriage became an increasingly uncomfortable place to be. After the Betjemans moved to Wantage in 1945, his wife, with a due sense of irony, opened a tea-shop. In the early 1960s Betjeman, now a passionate defender of England's past, made a series of films for regional television, including one about Bath. This became the basis for his involvement in the arguments of the late 1960s and early 1970s about the destruction of the "minor" architecture of Bath's heritage, and his often quoted complaints about "modern" architecture, including the "carbuncle" lecture theatre on the backside of the Bath Technical College. His poem "The Newest Bath Guide" was appended to *The Sack of Bath*:

> In those days of course there was not so much taste
> But now there's so much it has all run to waste
> In working out methods of cutting down cost -
> So that mouldings, proportion and texture are lost
> In a uniform nothingness. (this I first find
> In the terrible 'Tech' with its pointed behind.)

Presumably people have become used to the Tech and its carbuncle lecture theatre. It is a tribute to Betjeman's generosity of spirit that his own architectural preferences were for the exuberance of the

Victorians rather than the sobriety of the Georgians. It is perhaps a fitting tribute to him that Bath's Victorian heritage is now being given the attention it deserves.

And after Betjeman? Well, literature is alive and well in Bath, not least in the hands of the Bath Literature Festival and the Children's Literature Festival, as we shall see in the next chapter. The MA in Creative Writing at Bath Spa University both responds to local enthusiasm for writing but itself feeds into the pool of those hoping to join the ranks of published writers. Others prefer poetry as performance, which takes poetry back to its roots in pre-literate societies, and in drama. Poetry is actively promoted in the city by such authors as Susan Boyle and Nikki Bennett. There are regular talks and readings at the Bath Royal Literary and Scientific Institution in Queen Square and other venues around the town. Quite properly there is a concern for the quality of the written word. Yet there is also a troubling sense of the difficulty of finding subject matter that challenges the reader and addresses some of the harder themes of the new century. For the moment, it is straws in the wind: Rose Flint and Helen Moore have chosen to write about the environment and its protection; Dikra Ridha, an Iraqi-British poet living in Bath, reflects in her work the impact of international events and the closeness of the new, global world. The city is not a time-capsule, and our lives are entwined in forces that can be scarcely understood and which we observe helplessly from outside. All this is central to an understanding of twenty-first century Bath.

The recent Holburne Museum extension

6 | Visual Images
Art, Drama and Cinema

Bath is served by two major public art galleries, at either end of the vista that carries the eye from Pulteney Bridge down through Laura Place to Pulteney Street. The Victoria Art Gallery occupies a rather undistinguished late Victorian building which continues the line of the north end of the Guildhall extension. For many older Bathonians, the building is better known as the Bath public library, which occupied the ground floor from 1912 to 1990. Now this space is kept for temporary exhibitions, while the permanent collection is housed in the upper gallery, a large top-lit space with a rather pretentious cast of the Parthenon frieze which only serves to emphasize the relatively modest pictures. The gallery runs a successful "Adopt a Picture" scheme through which private individuals and businesses pay the cost of restoration in return for the right to hang the picture in a home or office—or even to leave them hanging in the gallery, as a few of these patrons of the visual arts have done.

At the other end of Pulteney Street is the Holburne Museum. The Holburne family came from Menstrie near Stirling, selling their castle and moving south in the late eighteenth century. By 1801 the family was established In Bath. William Holburne, who founded this very personal collection of pictures and artefacts, was in the navy and saw action at Trafalgar at the tender age of just twelve. From 1820 he and his three unmarried sisters lived at Cavendish Crescent and William began collecting. He completed the Grand Tour in 1824/5. The last surviving sister donated the collection on trust to the city in 1882, "to form the nucleus of a museum of fine art in Bath". Sir Reginald Blomfield was called in to oversee the conversion of the redundant Sydney Hotel into the new Holburne Museum, opened in 1916.

The building itself has the appearance of a fine Georgian mansion, neatly terminating the long, unencumbered view down Pulteney Street. Yet in many ways the "business" of the building had always been done at the rear. It faced onto the pleasure grounds of Sydney Gardens, where Jane Austen, who lived nearby, enjoyed breakfasts at one end of the day and fireworks at its close. There was a first-floor semi-circular loggia where an orchestra played at concerts. Even the chairmen were not forgotten, with a small bar—the Sydney Tap—in the basement where they could obtain refreshment and entertain themselves while their employers were strolling and chattering in the gardens.

By the 1960s the Holburne had fallen on hard times. Visitor numbers were low and reserves were being used to pay running costs. The view of the museum trustees, as Cathryn Spence described it in a *Bath Magazine* article, was that "only by extending the Holburne could it be made a community asset, appealing to the public as well as to the serious student." But this was exactly the period when the heritage movement was flexing its muscles in Bath. There were objections to any plans to build an extension to a Georgian building, especially if using a modern design. An alternative plan emerged with neoclassical wings added to the original hotel building. But by 1974 plans were abandoned and the caretaker's flat, converted to provide a gallery and a study room, became home to the Crafts Study Centre, opened in 1977. By the end of the century the Crafts Study Centre had moved to Farnham in Surrey where it now occupies a fine new building as part of the University for the Creative Arts. The Holburne was once more faced by a stark choice: decay or grow. The Holburne chose growth, and came up with a controversial plan for an ultramodern rear extension that would re-open the building to its original setting within the Sydney Gardens. Forty years on from the original extension plans the debate raged, publicly in the council chamber and in the columns of the *Bath Chronicle*, still in those days a daily evening paper, and privately within such organizations as the Bath Preservation Trust. Caroline Kay, the new chief executive of the Bath Preservation Trust "arrived in a storm" (her words) in 2007, of which the Holburne extension plan was a large part. The board was "split down the middle" and eventually took what she now sees as the "mature" decision that it was unable to reach a view on the desirability or otherwise of the new design by Eric Parry. The council said yes, and building began.

As with the new spa building, the Holburne extension answers the important question "how can you do good contemporary design in Bath?" In particular, it aims to restore the original pretension of the building to a light-hearted, almost witty, pastoral scene at the rear and a solid, serious and urban frontage. Unlike the new spa building, the work was completed on schedule in 2011. Much of Blomfield's work, especially moving the staircase to a central position within the house, has been unpicked, and there is great excitement. The axis of Great Pulteney Street continues visually through the museum and out into the gardens beyond. Visitors to the new galleries and its café are separated only by plate glass walls from the gardens and the new back entrance into the park. From key points in the building it is possible to view the panorama of Pulteney Street and then swivel through 180 degrees to take in the Sydney Gardens as well. Much of the Holburne collection consists of art objects, rather than paintings, and smaller spaces, including drawers and cupboards, enable these to be displayed more effectively. Greater space overall means that more ambitious temporary exhibitions will be held, and educational work increased. The new Holburne is an outstanding success.

Thomas Gainsborough

The most distinguished English painter who lived and worked in Bath was Thomas Gainsborough (1727-88), "this most likeable of men," as Nicola Kalinsky calls him. He loved music, owning five violas de gamba. He also loved glamorous young women. He painted the musical Linley sisters, not unaware of their startling beauty, in a sylvan glade, a picture now in the Dulwich Picture Gallery in South London. Their father Thomas organized entertainments at the Assembly Rooms, as well as being a major shareholder in the private Margaret Chapel in what is now Margaret's Buildings, between the Circus and Royal Crescent. Later Gainsborough painted a rather sad and dreamy portrait of Elizabeth ("Mrs Sheridan", 1785) now in the

National Gallery of Art in Washington DC. Her public singing career terminated on her notorious elopement with the playwright Sheridan and she worked alongside him at Drury Lane Theatre. From 1780 she was a "political wife" entertaining for her MP husband. It is another example of the phenomenon that we noted in the previous chapter, of the limitations placed on the professional careers of women in eighteenth-century England.

Bath was an excellent location for an artist wanting to develop a lucrative career as a portrait painter. Gainsborough lived here from 1759-74. His first studio was in an almost ideal location, in the Abbey Churchyard. The artist's studio was on the first floor; the ground floor shop was occupied from 1762 by his sister, a milliner. There was also a ground-floor showroom for the artist as well as a public passageway leading to the King's and Queen's Baths. The house, designed by John Wood, was demolished in 1890 during further excavations of the Roman Baths, and part of the site is now occupied by the eastward extension to the Pump Room. The Victoria has a pretty little 1796 Turner watercolour of the west front of Bath Abbey, which shows the buildings cluttering both north and south sides, including the one where Gainsborough worked. During this period Gainsborough painted Captain William Wade for the card room at the new Upper Assembly Rooms. Wade was Master of Ceremonies there from 1769 to 1777 when he left because of an affair with the wife of a visitor which led to him being named in a divorce suit. This picture has now found its way back to its intended place after being sold at the beginning of the twentieth century by the hard-up private owners of the Assembly Rooms, although it has to be said that its position high on the wall of the octagon room (where cards were played before the much grander card room was added) makes it extremely hard to see in detail.

Another picture which chimes neatly with the public life of Georgian Bath is the Holburne portrait of Dr. Rice Charleton, painted in 1764. It is a splendid and altogether credible image of a man at the height of his professional career. Dr. Charleton was the author of *A Treatise on the Bath Waters*, a key text in the ongoing debate about the medical efficacy of the spa waters, and senior physician at the General Hospital (later the Mineral Water Hospital) from 1757 to 1781. Charleton looked after the health of Gainsborough and his family throughout their Bath years and since Gainsborough paid his medical bills with pictures, the good doctor ended up with six landscapes and this full-length portrait. That the visits of the members of the Gainsborough family to the doctor were frequent and the bills large is reflected in the additional fact that Gainsborough painted two other Bath doctors: Dr. Abel Moysey and Dr. Ralph Schomberg.

It was not just the controversy about the Bath waters or his own personal tension between portraiture and landscape that is reflected in Gainsborough's work, but the growing debate about Britain's involvement in slavery and the slave trade. "The Byam Family" (1762-66) is sufficiently important to have been displayed at the National Gallery during the recent closure of the Holburne for refurbishment. This life-size view of a wealthy English family enjoying the countryside is one of the most impressive and ambitious paintings made by Thomas Gainsborough during his fifteen years in Bath. It was the centrepiece of a 2001 exhibition at the Holburne, with a lavish and extensive catalogue entitled *Love's Prospect: Gainsborough's 'Byam Family' and the Eighteenth Century Marriage Portrait*. The essay by Hugh Belsey on "Antigua, Surrey and Bath: Gainsborough and the Byam family" makes both the general point that Bath was the "perfect market for any portrait painter"—people with leisure and money—but also confirms the specific link with slavery. George Byam was born in Antigua where his family had owned sugar plantations since the mid-seventeenth century. By 1763 they had 366 acres, worked by 132 slaves. By this time George was away in England, enjoying the pleasures of Bath, before eventually settling in very English Surrey in 1766 with his wife Louisa Bathurst. The picture reached Bath in 1998 after a rather circuitous journey via Marlborough College and the Andrew Brownsword Arts Foundation. (Brownsword is a wealthy entrepreneur and was the owner of Bath Rugby Club from 1996-2010.)

In 1766 Gainsborough, now an established artist, moved up to The Circus away from the bustle of central Bath and the steam from the hot spring waters. He had a north-facing studio at the back of his house. An important aspect of the Victoria Art Gallery's collection is the light it casts on what Bath actually looked like at various points in its history. To appreciate what The Circus looked like at this period, John Robert Cozens' dramatic view of 1773 hangs in the Victoria. It shows a huge empty space crossed by a couple of coaches, two sedan chairs and a few pedestrians. While the giant plane trees that now occupy that open space are much loved by both locals and visitors, the picture does suggest that something has been lost as nature has reasserted itself beyond human design. An earlier picture in the Victoria, "Ladymead House", painted about 1730 by an unknown artist, shows a large three-storey house with four gables above dating from the 1680s. It is surrounded by extensive ornamental gardens and an orchard, sloping down to the River Avon. Even more remarkable is that the house still stands in Ladymead, the central section of Walcot Street, a rare survivor of the pre-Georgian architecture of the lost Cotswold city of Bath. Having served as a penitentiary (refuge) for prostitutes in Victorian times, for much of the twentieth century it was used as a council home for elderly women. Unfortunately, there is now little of the pre-Georgian to be seen, at least externally, and the house looks large and a little bleak.

Joseph Farington's "The Royal Crescent" has the river in the foreground and the light shining on unpolluted Bath stone up above. Farington was best known as a diarist in London, where he kept an account of his life and doings from 1793 to 1821. Bath, as we have noted, began to change and grow rapidly in the Victorian period. John Syer's "View of Bath from the South East", painted in 1846, looks across the city from a high vantage point, much like the modern view from the delightful allotments in Abbey View, Widcombe. It shows Georgian and Regency Bath in its complete form, right up to St. Stephen's church on Lansdown and the terraces out along the London Road. An important addition to the central scene is the spire of St. John's Roman Catholic Church, competing with and higher than the abbey tower. The railway is there, albeit playing a minor role in the bottom left corner. Twerton mills lurk among the smoke and mist in the middle distance. High above,

Kelston Knoll stands out with its familiar clump of trees already on top. It is hard to believe that over 150 years have passed. Other images of Georgian and Regency Bath may be seen at the Museum of Costume in the Assembly Rooms, the Museum of Bath at Work, and at 1 The Royal Crescent, the headquarters of the Bath Preservation Trust.

Photography

In keeping with its status as a place of scientific curiosity from the mid-eighteenth century onwards, Bath has a small but distinguished place in the history of photography. It is still the home of the Royal Photographic Society, although in recent years the society has been forced by financial pressures to abandon its tenancy of the Octagon Chapel in Milsom Street for the rather more modest surroundings of the Wells Road on the southern outskirts. During the 1980s and 1990s the Octagon provided an impressive and sympathetic exhibition space, but such is now the ubiquity of the photograph that it seems that insufficient members of the public were prepared to pay to simply "look at photos".

It was very different in the early nineteenth century when William Henry Fox Talbot was carrying out his early experiments at Lacock Abbey, just across the border into Wiltshire. The career of Fox Talbot, elected a Fellow of the Royal Society in 1831 at the age of only 31, suggests that we may devalue the actual scientific and technical achievements of such "gentlemen scholars". To call such a man an amateur is to underestimate the painstaking and systematic way in which he advanced slowly towards the invention of photography in the 1830s and 1840s. It is moving to see at first hand the actual places revealed in these early photographs, including the fine architecture of Lacock Abbey itself, and such everyday objects as Firefoot, the children's galloping rocking horse, fondly remembered in later years by younger members of the family. Now Lacock Abbey rests with the National Trust and there is a fine permanent exhibition of Fox Talbot and the history of photography. In 1889 Charles Henry Talbot, William's son, presented a hand-selected album of his father's prints to the Bath Photographic Society. Sadly, they were sold at auction in 1975, and to the best of my knowledge no-one intervened to save this record for the city. The material that was once in the hands of the Royal Photographic Society is now at the National Media Museum in Bradford, Yorkshire.

Bath on Stage

According to William Lowndes, the historian of Bath's Theatre Royal, Bath was regularly visited by travelling players in the sixteenth and seventeenth centuries. We know that they played the Guildhall at least once, in 1626, though more commonly performances were held in the courtyards of inns, with the spectators watching from windows and balconies. The first purpose-built theatre was in Parsonage Lane, but as Bath became a fashionable resort it quickly proved too small and in any case was demolished when the Bath General Hospital was put up in 1736. It was not until 1750 that a new theatre opened in Orchard Street, close to the Lower (Simpson's) Assembly Rooms and the fashionable Parades.

Plans for the new theatre involved many of the establishment figures in eighteenth-century Bath whose names recur in this book. Orchard Street takes its name from the site of the old abbey orchard, purchased by John Wood (developer and architect) in partnership with James Leake (bookseller and small-time pornographer). Beau Nash was a shareholder in the venture, which was led by John Hippesley, a Bristol actor. Hippesley's prospectus included the supposition that fashionable Bath was a place "where might reasonably be expected (next to London) the best Theatre in England". The current management would no doubt wish to echo those words.

John Palmer took on the task of developing what was to become St. James' Theatre. A word must be said at this point about the name John Palmer, since no fewer than four men of this name played important roles in Bath in the second half of the eighteenth century. Only two were related—the father and son who between them built up the theatre. They are not to be confused with John Palmer the actor or John Palmer, city architect. More confusion is created by the fact that the John Palmer junior of the theatre was also a mail coach entrepreneur, and later both Mayor of Bath and one of its MPs.

Furthermore, John Palmer the architect was responsible for both the extension of the Orchard Street theatre in 1775 and the new Theatre Royal of 1802-5. I hope that is clear.

For the first six years of its life, St. James' Theatre was in competition with plays put on at the nearby Simpson's Assembly Rooms. Eventually Beau Nash engineered a deal by which the theatre would put on only plays (no dancing) and Simpson's only music and dancing (no plays). All of this seems a long time ago, and the theatre has not functioned as a theatre in nearly 200 years, Yet it is still possible to visit the "old" theatre, and see the 1774 solid stone stage, the remains of a stage box, the incredibly narrow backstage area where scenery was hung from the wall rather than set up on the stage and the high vault with its ventilation system (theatre audiences were no cleaner or less smelly than most of our ancestors). In the basement it is also possible to see the original outflow from the King's Bath. In its subsequent history, Orchard Street has served as Bath's main Roman Catholic Chapel, and subsequently its Masonic Hall, but this part of the remarkable and varied history of this building belongs in Chapter 8.

Under the skilful management of the Palmers, Bath quickly became an important provincial centre of the English stage. In 1768, it was the first theatre outside London to receive royal approval and the right to call itself "Theatre Royal". It witnessed outstanding performances by actors of the star quality of David Garrick and Sarah Siddons, and plays by contemporary authors such as Richard Sheridan and Hannah More. Gainsborough painted Mrs. Siddons as did Sir Joshua Reynolds ("Mrs. Siddons as The Tragic Muse", 1784). While Reynolds emphasizes her dramatic persona, in Gainsborough's picture she is still, and her face inscrutable. When she returned to the Bath stage from London in 1799, her performance caused a riot, since the management at Orchard Street, determined to cash in on its most famous daughter, sold far more tickets than could be accommodated in the theatre.

Bath had moved on, and fashionable Bath had emigrated northwards. It was here, between the old town and Queen Square that a new Theatre Royal, designed by the fashionable London architect

George Dance the Younger, was opened in 1805. The work was supervised by John Palmer, the city architect. Not least the new theatre enabled Bath to keep up with Bristol, where the fine Georgian theatre dates from 1766. Siddons played the new theatre in 1807 and 1808, while plays came and went between Bath (the testing-ground) and London. Sheridan's *School for Scandal* played at Bath a year after its first performance at Drury Lane. Meanwhile, Bath grew, but in ways that reduced its distinctiveness as a city of leisure. Rather it became a relatively workaday town, albeit with a large retirement population. One of the growth industries in Bath was religion, and as we shall see in Chapter 8, many new churches were built in the city. The Puritanism that had long been the other face of amoral, happy-go-lucky Bath now came to the fore. In the 1840s the rector of St. Michael's described the theatre as "a dangerous enemy to virtue and happiness", much as Hannah More, fifty years earlier, had set aside her early career writing for the theatre for the more serious business of writing morally improving pamphlets.

As so often happens, it needed a disaster to provoke a renewal of theatrical life in Bath. That disaster was the fire of 1862, closely followed by the decision to rebuild, a feat achieved in under a year. A sixteen-year-old unknown, Ellen Terry, played Titania in *A Midsummer Night's Dream* at the opening night. The theatre was given a new Italianate entrance on Sawclose, and the lovely late Georgian original façade on Beaufort Square retired into obscurity until rescued, cleaned and restored at the end of the twentieth century.

The British theatre was on the up towards the end of the nineteenth century, with new dramatists such as Shaw, Wilde and Barrie. Attitudes towards Wilde were ambivalent, and when *A Woman of No Importance* played at Bath in 1896, only a few months after Wilde's shameful imprisonment in Reading jail, his name was left off the playbill. Opera, musical comedy and Gilbert and Sullivan were also in the repertoire, although opera was both expensive and not entirely to the Bath taste, as the Bath Festival organizers were to discover some years later. Yet by the middle of the last century, faced by competition from both cinema and television, the shabby old Theatre Royal with its splintering wooden benches up in the gods, was in a bad way. In my own youth, I remember pantomime—and little else. As Lowndes writes: "Regrettably, it was said, only pantomime, local amateur productions, Agatha Christie plays and Sooty, the one-man puppet show that had won spectacular fame on television, could guarantee capacity houses."

Yet interest in culture in every sense was growing in the city as new and different sorts of people bought into the dream of life in the Queen of the West and the lovely surrounding countryside. In 1979 a charitable trust headed by Jeremy Fry, a prominent figure in the Bath Festival, bought the theatre and registered it as a charity. There was a public appeal for funds, and Bath City Council donated £400,000 from the £1.7 million it had received from the sale to Sainsbury's of a hundred-year lease on Green Park Station—a price no doubt inflated by a competitive bid from Tesco. The Arts Council chipped in, as did other local authorities, while the Bath Preservation Trust contributed to the restoration of the original Beaufort Square façade.

So what of the Theatre Royal today? After another major refurbishment in 2010, the theatre reopened with a well received production of Sheridan's "Bath" play, *The Rivals*. The theatre seems to be on a permanent wave of success. It has a unique status that reflects its early history of working closely with London theatres, as theatre boss Danny Moar explained in conversation with Somerset novelist and playwright Crysse Morrison:

> Theatre Royal Bath is a registered charity, but we set up a producing company which is called Theatre Royal Bath Productions, and in ten years we've put on about ninety productions. What's interesting about our operation is that we not only produce plays but we produce them commercially, and the money the production company generates goes to pay for all our not-for-profit activities—the children's theatre, the studio space, and the education department. I don't know anywhere else this is happening in one organisation.

Theatre Royal Productions promotes new productions, the most successful of which are then toured to other provincial theatres or transferred to the London West End, in a reversal of the relationship between Bath and London existing through most of the Theatre Royal's history. In recent years the Peter Hall Company has run a repertoire season in summer which means that year-round live theatre is now available in Bath. But not all is new; Shakespeare still plays in Bath, there is Gilbert and Sullivan still, and Shaw, Wilde and Noel Coward are still among the most frequently performed playwrights. Perhaps the cutting edge of the theatre is now the Ustinov Studio and the Young People's Theatre, called the egg, with its wide-ranging educational programme.

Theatre spreads like a contagious disease in Bath. Suddenly fashionable Larkhall, off the London Road, has its Rondo Theatre. It is a theatre that has many enthusiastic, committed *aficionados*, and is similar in feel to the pub theatres which have grown in number in nearby Bristol in recent years. Meanwhile, Corn Street, opposite the Avon Street car-park, has its Mission Theatre. There is a resident Next Stage Theatre Company, while the venue also puts on music shows and that holy grail of Bath theatre—opera. Both the Bath Comedy Festival and the Bath Fringe Festival use the Mission as a venue. Those with a certain sense of history-as-irony will enjoy the thought that just as the old Mission Hall where the theatre is based sought to bring religion to this traditional slum area of town, so the Mission Theatre seeks to extend still further the tentacles of culture in the city. Another important site for festival performances is the Chapel Arts Centre in Lower Borough Walls. This hosts a wide range of performing arts, including music of all kinds, theatre, dance, comedy, film, poetry and multimedia shows. In addition they offer workshops and rehearsal spaces.

Chapel Arts is just one a of a number of venues used by the School of Performing Arts at Bath Spa University, which uses it as a teaching space and puts on up to twenty performances there a year. This new university has grown from the teacher training college at Newton Park, an estate just to the west of Bath. One of the college's special strengths was music, but this has now developed in ways which would have been difficult to predict fifty years ago. Classical concerts are put on at the Michael Tippett Centre at Newton Park, but also at venues big (for example, the Assembly Rooms and abbey) and small (Mission Theatre) around the city. The music is much more diverse now, covering classical, contemporary, world and rock-'n'roll. Bands play at local clubs and pubs, while in 2010 the university signed a deal to develop a major new venue at Birdall's Yard on London Road in an area of social deprivation but with considerable potential for regeneration. Some of these students will move on but others will stay in the area and add to the cultural liveliness of the city. Meanwhile, Bath University does not ignore the arts completely: a new Arts Complex will open in 2014, and the university is home to the Institute of Contemporary Interdisciplinary Arts, with an exciting and developing programme of performances, projects and exhibitions.

Public Art and Film

One of the more unusual exhibits in the Victoria Art Gallery in the summer of 2010 was a sculpture of a lion, decorated with graffiti by the artist Peter Blake, one of a hundred such highly coloured sculptures scattered round the city. It contained the names of such luminaries of the rock'n'roll world as Chuck Berry and Elvis Presley and landmarks such as Michael Eavis' Glastonbury Festival. Lions have pedigree in Bath. The lion on the city coat-of-arms represents the coronation of King Edgar at Bath Abbey in 973, over one thousand years ago. The three lions badge, so familiar from its use by England football teams, was adopted by King Richard the Lionheart and the inn sign outside Bath's smallest pub, the Coeur-de-Lion in Northumberland Place, shows Richard riding into battle with the three lions emblazoned on his shield. Two very fierce bronze lion sculptures mark the entrance to the Royal Victoria Park at the city end, just off Gay Street and a stone's throw from the Jane Austen centre.

A number of coincidences are at work here. Firstly the fine restoration of the Victoria Park lions to their splendid Victorian best, secondly the public expectations behind the England football team as it set off for the World Cup finals, and thirdly the enormous popular success of King Bladud's Pigs in 2008. This public art project raised a staggering £200,000 towards the cost of the Two Tunnels project which will connect Bath by cycle and pedestrian path to the valleys south of the city. Film director Ken Loach, a resident of the city and a football fanatic, got in on the act too. Three of the lions were unveiled to the public at Twerton Park, home of Bath City Football Club, of which Loach has been a director in the past and remains a loyal supporter. Dressed in his trademark leather jacket and open neck shirt, the film director, despite the disclaimer that he was "no artist", added the Bath City logo to the one called "Lionheart", designed by local artist Justina Benson and decorated by schoolchildren.

Loach's contribution to culture in Bath is not confined to drawing logos on sculpted lions. He has made one short documentary film about Bath, or to be more accurate, about Bath City Football Club: *The Other City*. Centred on the football club out at Twerton, the title implicitly suggests a contrast between the Bath of the large, fashionable rugby club playing on the Recreation Ground in the heart of the world heritage city, and the modest Bath of the much smaller football club playing among the council estates at Twerton Park. Loach has become almost the Beckford of contemporary Bath, a resident but detached from much of the fashionable clamour and noise of the city. It is no surprise that Beckford's Tower dominates the splendid view from the terraces of the football club while the football ground can be seen very clearly from the top of the tower.

A number of benefit performances of Loach films have been held in the Little Theatre in Bath, including *My Name is Joe* and *The Wind that Shakes the Barley*. More recently, *Land and Freedom* (his film about the Spanish Civil War) was shown at the Victoria Art Gallery in conjunction with an exhibition of the work of war photographer Don McCullin. The beneficiary is of course Bath City Football Club. Other Loach films have been shown at the social club at Twerton Park, supported by both football fans and members of the Bath Film Society and Bath University Film Society. Usually Loach comes accompanied by one of the actors from the film in question. Film, for Loach, is very much a team game.

In 2009 the Loach film that everyone was talking about was *Eric*. Loach came with the film for a showing at the Little Theatre.

Bath city centre from the south (*above*);
River Avon at North Parade Bridge (*below*)

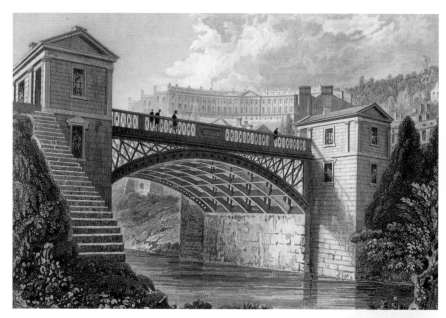

Cleveland Bridge, 1830, with Camden Crescent above (*above*); Gorgon's Head from the Temple of Sul Minerva, Roman Baths Museum (*right*); Heritage Museum of the North Somerset Coal Industry, Radstock (*below*)

Opposite:
The Great Bath and Bath Abbey (*top*);
Bath Abbey from High Street (*bottom*)

3

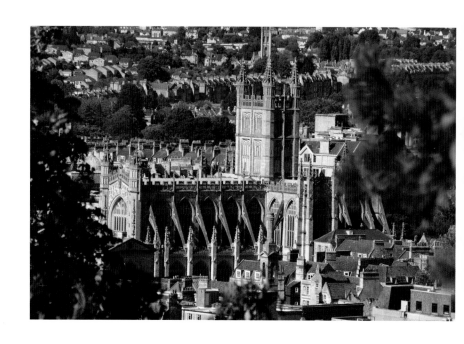

Bath Abbey from the south-west (*above*)
Thermae Bath Spa (*below*)

Pump Room Terrace, 1914 (*above*)
The Royal Crescent and the Bath Skyline (*below*)

The Royal
Crescent (*right*)

Detail of the Doric frieze at The
Circus (*left*); Provincial Baroque?:
Rosewell House, Kingsmead Square
(*below left*); Pulteney Bridge (*below
right*)

Abbey Green with plane-tree and Crystal Palace pub
(*above*); Ralph Allen's townhouse (*right*); The Pump Room,
1864 (*below*)

A View of the Parade at Bath, c.1787 (now North Parade)

NORTH PARADE P.ᵗᵉ POINT-STREET

..DE AT BATH.

The crowded slums of Avon Street *(above)*
Stall Street colonnade with Pump Room and Abbey, looking from Bath Street, 1864 *(below)*

Gainsborough, Mrs. Sheridan (Elizabeth Linley), 1785 (*left*)

Jane Austen Museum, Gay Street *(right)*
Theatre Royal Bath (*below left*)
Parade Gardens (*below right*)

(*clockwise from top left*) Museum of Bath at Work (originally an eighteenth-century real tennis court); St Michael's Without Church (Church of England); Jewish cemetery, Combe Down; St. John the Evangelist Church (Roman Catholic); Bath City Football Club at Twerton Park

(*above, left to right*) Bladud, Adelard, Bath Oliver biscuits

Richard (Beau) Nash,
1740
(*left*)

Caroline Herschel

Caroline Herschel, a portrait of 1829 (*above*)
The Herschel Museum of Astronomy *(right)*

The Buff Club at the Pig and Whistle, Avon Street, 1825 (*above*)
The Bath Blitz, 1942 (*below*)

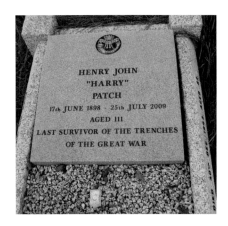

Harry Patch's gravestone, Monkton Combe (*above left*); Widcombe Mummers, Abbey Churchyard, St. George's Day, 2010 (*above right*)
Eagle House, Batheaston (*below*)

The American Museum, Claverton Manor (*bottom left*)
Beckford's Tower, Lansdown (*bottom right*)

He also came with Big Eric, alias French international footballer Eric Cantona, who plays a central role in the film. Hundreds of football fans paid to attend a question-and-answer session at Twerton Park, and to have their photos taken with the great man. For a football club which at that point was averaging crowds of fewer than one thousand, it was a very big occasion indeed.

Film has been around in Bath for nearly one hundred years now. Between the world wars, the Assembly Rooms were pressed into use as a cinema. In the 1950s and 1960s Bath boasted the Beau Nash in Westgate Street and the Odeon in Southgate Street. Both of these are gone now, the Odeon swept away by the first of the Southgate redevelopments, the Beau Nash replaced by newer cinemas, most recently the multiscreen cinema in James Street West. The most splendid of them all was the art deco Forum at the junction of St. James' Parade and Southgate Street. As cinema audiences declined in the 1970s and 1980s, this became used by an evangelical church and as an occasional venue for classical concerts in the ongoing absence of a proper concert hall in the city. Surprisingly, the Little Theatre fared better. It had always been the "flea-pit", a small cinema showing the films the big cinemas did not want. But as Bath became a student city, with new audiences for films different from the Hollywood mainstream, the Little has become the success story of Bath cinemas, with further screens miraculously appearing in hidden recesses of the building.

The Bath area has become a popular place in which to make films, and has a local government department dedicated to promoting this role: the Bath Film Office. Apart from feature films, it also promotes the use of various Bath locations for advertisements and other promotional films. The new Bath Spa has proved especially popular for this purpose, while the Pump Room and Roman Baths continue to be used.

One of the first and best loved feature films made around Bath was the Ealing comedy *The Titfield Thunderbolt* (1952) set along the route of the recently closed Somerset Coal Railway in the Cam valley. Rather at the other end of the film spectrum, the Pump Room became the Moscow Conservatoire for Ken Russell's 1970 film about the troubled Russian composer Tchaikovsky. Then there were the various well-known (even notorious?) television adaptations of Jane Austen stories … Did Bath do more, one might ask, than contribute to the cult of the period film or television romance? It is a matter of straws in the wind.

In addition to films which have drawn on Bath's pretty Georgian and Regency settings, a few films have attempted to tackle more difficult issues in historical settings. Suri Krishnamma's *A Respectable Trade* (BBC, 1997) was a tale of love and personal greed and ambition set against the backdrop of Bristol's (and Bath's) part in the eighteenth-century slave trade. North Parade Buildings and The Circus both feature in the film. Saul Dibb's 2008 film, *The Duchess*, is based on the life of Georgina Cavendish, Duchess of Devonshire. An account of aristocratic life and morals in the eighteenth century, it was almost inevitable that at least some of the scenes would be set in Bath. Gambling, adultery and over-indulgence in wine are among the vices enjoyed by the duchess. In 2003 Mira Nair used Bath extensively for the outdoor scenes of *Vanity Fair*, her adaptation of Thackeray's novel. The social rise of Becky Sharp in a corrupt society, and her corruption in the process, is another sharp reminder of some of the more unpleasant aspects of "polite" society in Bath which have occasionally raised their inquiring heads in the pages of this book.

Parade Gardens

7 | Leisure and Pleasure
Popular Culture and Pastimes

Bath is sleepy on a Sunday afternoon in summer, and what better place to snooze away the afternoon than the Parade Gardens, right in the heart of the city. The grass is green and lush, there are enough trees for those who like their summers a little shady, there are splendid flower beds in the best traditions of municipal planting schemes. There is even a lion, a large green lion, made almost entirely of house-leeks and standing sturdily upon a flower bed with the red cross of St. George on a white background (begonias, I think).

There is a pleasant café in the corner furthest from the entrance on Grand Parade, which seems to make much of local produce. The buildings of Bath sit round demurely in a semi-circle—South Parade, Bog Island, the tower of the abbey with its fluttering flag, the Guildhall, the Empire Hotel. Even this most ghastly of Bath buildings has now been here so long that it looks comfortable and at home. Some say that putting such a building in such a prominent position was a punishment by Major Davis, the City Architect, for some slight by the city fathers. Maybe, but a sunny summer Sunday is no time to be pernickety.

The Eating and Drinking City

Brewing has a long historical profile in Bath. In addition to his better-known postal and quarrying activities, Ralph Allen set up a brewery and malthouse at the Dolmeads in 1736. By 1793 there were twelve breweries and by 1850 there were 34. Amalgamations and the growth of large-scale national breweries producing a standardized product with only a vague connection with real ale had more or less destroyed brewing in Bath by the middle of the twentieth century. But changing tastes and changing attitudes to food and drink have begun to favour the local again. Abbey Ales brew their prize-winning Bellringer in the city and own both the Star and the Coeur-de-Lion in Northumberland Place, only a stone's throw from the abbey.

"Too many pubs" has always been the complaint in Bath. Sometimes there is startling evidence of the "drink problem", seen on the streets on any Friday or Saturday evening; other evidence is gathered in Andrew Swift and Kirsten Eliott's magnificent trilogy on the pubs of Bath. In *The Lost Pubs of Bath* they tell the story about the White Hart in Twerton High Street, taken over in 1899 by the zealots of a pseudo-Masonic group called the Good Templars. Any alcoholic drinks found in the pub were poured away, fixtures related to running a pub broken and the place re-opened as a teetotal meeting-place and restaurant. Now the building is neither pub nor teetotal centre, yet at first floor level it is still possible to read the words "White Hart Templar Institute and Restaurant Twerton Lodge", together with the words they were meant to cover up: "Wines and Spirits".

It is really startling that there are sufficient closed pubs in Bath to justify a whole book on the subject, and it would be interesting to know of other towns and cities that have inspired such a volume and the dedicated research needed to write it. Of course, death and resurrection go together with pubs and one which has re-opened its doors is the Royal Oak on the Lower Bristol Road. Now the building sits comfortably by the roadside as it has done since the late eighteenth century. But for one hundred years from 1874 it had the Somerset and Dorset Railway viaduct passing just a few feet from its first floor windows, with heavy goods and passenger trains trundling by on a regular basis until closure of the line in the 1960s and the eventual demolition of the viaduct. The pub closed in 2002, survived attempts to have it demolished and re-opened in 2005 after extensive and loving restoration. It is now a haven of real ale and cider in the city and hopefully the students who now inhabit this part of town in increasing numbers will keep it in business for many years to come.

One pub more or less is a normal occurrence in any city, but for some communities out of the centre, the closure of a local pub may be a shattering experience. Such a pub was the Retreat, in a semi-rural area on the north side of the city between Sion Hill and Primrose Hill, where the ground begins to rise steeply towards Lansdown. Swift and Elliott describe it as "Bath's most missed pub". A garden inventory of 1879 which they reproduce does suggest a rather special kind of place: "Double light cucumber frame, greenhouse with grape vine, 36 currant trees, 7 fruit trees, 2 rows of raspberries, heap of manure, shrub and rose trees, rustic stones forming edging to garden, two large forms."The present owners have left the front more or less unchanged and it is still possible to look through the gate, see the winding path between flower beds, the outside wrought-iron balcony with shady benches beneath. The most striking feature of this pub was that it had no road access. A path led from Sion Hill with high walls on either side but sufficiently wide to roll beer barrels along. Beyond it the path descended via a steep flight of steps into Primrose Hill and thence to Weston. When I first went there, as a teenager and often after evensong at St. John's Lower Weston on a Sunday evening, we were only permitted to use the balcony, with strict instructions from landlord Richard Gawith that if the police arrived, we were to wait for them to enter the pub, then slip down into the lane beside the pub and make our escape across the fields. It never happened. The only drink allowed was ordinary bitter which I still find myself referring to as "boys' bitter". Later, Dick allowed us into the bar and we learned the rules and etiquette of such pub games as shove ha'penny and cribbage. Despite his uncertain temper, this landlord had a lot to teach the world about "responsible drinking". With a keen sense of timing, Dick died two days before the pub closed. In 1991 the then owners hosted a grand reunion at which Dick's widow Nora presided. Two days later, she too died.

Within the city centre, the visitor or newcomer to the city will do well to remember that size is not everything in pubs. In the alleys and passageways of Bath the discerning drinker can still find the Coeur-de-Lion and the Volunteer Rifleman's Arms. In Green Street, the Old Green Tree is still worth a visit, with its large variety of real ales and ciders and elegant floor to ceiling wooden panelling. But it is small, very small, and not the place for a private chat. You will almost certainly end up sharing a conversation with your fellow drinkers, especially if it is a match day for Bath Rugby. One other small pub is worth a mention here, the Salamander. Older Bathonians will remember this as Bath's first coffee bar, in the late 1950s. From that it progressed to a rather up-market bar, and is now the flagship pub of Bath Ales, a brewery located between Bath and Bristol. It also owns the Hop Pole on the Upper Bristol Road, a hop, skip and a jump from the Royal Victoria Park and the Royal Crescent.

Pubs have a certain survival rate, at least in a student and tourist city like Bath. This is less true of restaurants, which come and go according to trends and fashions. But one at least has lasted down the years—the Hole in the Wall in George Street. Small, friendly and extremely good, it first came to my notice as a sixth-former in Bath when we were seconded to help the City Council conduct a traffic census in the years leading up to the Buchanan Report and everything that came after. Working on the Upper Bristol Road in the middle of the evening on a Friday (or maybe Saturday) three cars we stopped in a row all gave as their destination The Hole in the Wall. So what was the big attraction? The answer, in one word, was Europe. What Elizabeth David did for English cooking by introducing continental ingredients and recipes into the English kitchen, the Hole in the Wall did for the restaurant trade. Framed on the wall is a hand-written menu from the early 1960s featuring such foreign delicacies as *aillade toulousaine*, *charcuterie*, mussels and scallops, apples cooked in butter and calvados, apricot *soufflé* and so on. There was even *paella* (42/-, or 42 shillings, or just over £2) which the owners felt it necessary to warn the world was "a Spanish risotto of chicken and shellfish". Needless to say it was a world to discover for the young man asking polite questions of the travelling public on the Upper Bristol Road.

There are, of course, the big set-piece places to eat such as the Royal Crescent Hotel and the Bath Priory, and the Lansdown Grove and Combe Grove hotels. There is certainly money in food and drink nowadays. In 2010 Hall and Woodhouse, the modest Blandford Forum brewery firm, opened their new restaurant in the old

Bonham's Auction Rooms, just off Queen Square. The total cost of the refurbishment was £6.2 million, which sounds like an awful lot of business lunches and tourist dinners, even in a relatively large dining area. Quite close to Hall and Woodhouse, in Quiet Street, the Eastern Eye has taken over an impressive early nineteenth-century bazaar and auction room. The restaurant occupies the lovely exhibition hall space on the first floor, with three shallow domes to the ceiling. There are three lavish Indian murals on musical themes the full length of one wall.

Cafés have a long history in Bath. Introduce a little food and drink into a Roman bath-house, let the water out, add a few news-papers and you are in eighteenth-century Bath. Even to the point of providing separate facilities for men and women to repair to after the ritual of the morning bathe and the drinking of spa water in the Pump Room. Fast forward a little and you are in Betjeman's Bath tea-shop and we can add encounters between the sexes to the rich mixture of café life. Personally, I miss Monk's in the Abbey Churchyard, but Sally Lunn's in Lilliput Alley is still there, in a tiny house, reputed to be the oldest in the city. As for the eponymous bun, the Sally Lunn, it is not English at all, but French, a version of the *brioche* introduced by a Huguenot (Protestant) refugee called Solange Luyon who came to work at a baker's shop in Lilliput Alley in the late seventeenth century. Hot and buttered, and extremely popular in Georgian Bath, the true Sally Lunn is quite different from the sugary buns usually sold as "Bath buns".

But to be truly in Bath and of Bath, there is only one place to go—the Pump Room. Here, tea and coffee are served morning and afternoon to the accompaniment, more often than not, of a discreet string quartet playing quietly in the background. The really brave can ask the waiter to bring them (at no extra charge) a glass of the warm, pungent spa water. And there is lunch too, not cheap, but who would expect it to be in these splendid eighteenth-century surroundings? On my most recent visit, St. George's Day 2010, to celebrate the ninetieth birthday of a dear Bath friend, there was additional enter-tainment. Before lunch there was a French choir singing traditional French music. And during our meal—this was after all St. George's

Day—the Widcombe Mummers paraded past in the Abbey Churchyard, performing the play of St. George in various places around the city. For once, I felt agreeably proud of my native city.

The Park City

In the eighteenth century public gardens were private. Admission was by payment (rather like the Parade Gardens today), and by definition the majority of the public excluded. These included the Sydney Gardens and, from the 1730s until the 1790s, Spring Gardens, accessed by ferry across the river, was a popular place of pleasure in the lower part of the city. We have seen already the shift in later Georgian Bath to a more sober, moralizing approach to life. Certainly the nineteenth century valued work and thrift. But there was also a recognition that people, working people that is, needed access to fresh air and exercise. The idea of good leisure, and of the park, was born.

The Royal Victoria Park, developed in the late 1820s, responded to a complex set of ideas about leisure and pleasure. It is also an educational park, the western end dominated by the Botanical Gardens with their sedate beds, classical summer-house and water feature. The fun element of the original conception owes something to Beckford—in particular the two dells on the western side of the parks, where I used to play happily for many hours as a small boy. They were magical places, but I had no consciousness of their special historical significance. Developed from old quarries, and elaborately designed with tree planting and the giant Jupiter head emerging incongruously from the surrounding shrubbery near the northern gates of the Botanic Gardens, they lend a suitably mysterious and "gothic" atmosphere to this corner of the park. Such playful elements contrast with more "imperial" features reflecting the progress of Victoria's reign, such as the obelisk and the triumphal archway into Marlborough Lane.

The Victoria Park was the site of the 1909 pageant, a vast community effort which presented excited visitors with a series of tableaux of Bath's history across the centuries from King Bladud and his pigs onwards. There were plenty of opportunities for dressing up, still rather an obsession with certain fragments of Bath society. The Bath pageant also met one of the original aims of the Victoria Park, which was to woo visitors back to Bath. Other frequent users of the Victoria Park in the twentieth century were circuses and military tattoos. While military tattoos seem to have dwindled in popularity, circuses continue to visit the park, although there is a ban on the use of performing animals on council land. Such events normally take place on the Middle Common, bounded by a narrow circular road. A major user is the early summer Bath Spring Flower Show which traditionally lights up this stretch of green grass. It is good to report that Bath was one of the few places in England that celebrated the centenary in 2008 of the 1908 Small Holdings and Allotments Act, still the main legal basis of the newly popular allotments movement.

Another much-frequented part of the park used for public events is the area below the Royal Crescent. During and after the Second World War it was briefly used for allotments. Now it hosts events such as open-air theatre, hot-air balloon launches and parades of pigs and lions. It was also the chosen venue for the Three Tenors concert, with community singing and fireworks, which celebrated prematurely the opening of the new Spa buildings. Until recently it hosted the opening Friday night celebrations of the Bath Music Festival. This became a very big party indeed during the 1990s, and as late as 2003 it provided over four hours of musical entertainment, rounded off with fireworks at 10pm. Sadly this is no longer.

The Museum City

There is no museum of Bath. While it would be helpful to have one place where all the strands of its history were gathered together, it may well be a blessing in disguise. It means that less fashionable aspects of Bath are dealt with more thoroughly than they might be as part of a general museum. The downside is that fewer visitors get to see the exhibits, and that they pay more for their museum visits. Location is everything here.

The Bath Postal Museum, which celebrates among other things the contributions of Ralph Allen (of Prior Park and the stone quarries) and John Palmer (of Orchard Street theatre) to the history of the British post, is on the old General Post Office site in Northgate Street and very central indeed. On the other hand, the quite fascinating Herschel Museum of Astronomy is tucked away in a rather anonymous house (Herschel's own home) in New King Street to the west of the city centre. Nevertheless, it is worth the detour. It presents very clearly the intertwined lives of William and his sister Caroline, both in their original profession as musicians, and their later lives as astronomers. Indeed, the museum is noteworthy for emphasizing that women as well as men were involved in scientific work in the later eighteenth century.

The Herschel Museum is one of four museums run by the Bath Preservation Trust. The others are No. 1 Royal Crescent, which presents a Georgian house much as it might have looked in the eighteenth century with much fine furniture and many interesting pictures, the Building of Bath Collection in the Countess of Huntingdon Chapel, and Beckford's Tower up on Lansdown. The one museum that every visitor to Bath gets to see is the Roman Baths, but two other much visited council-run collections are the Victoria Art Gallery and the Museum of Costume (or Fashion Museum) in the Assembly Rooms. Because of its location the Fashion Museum also attracts more general visitors who want the opportunity to visit this remarkable and much restored relic of a bygone age. Nearby is the Museum of East Asian Art, which celebrates very different cultural traditions. Like the Holburne and the American Museum at Claverton, it has all the charm of a personal collection, that of Brian McElney. In a tight narrow house facing across to the Assembly Rooms, it incorporates a temporary gallery and shop on the ground floor, with two floors above featuring ceramics, metal goods, jade and porcelain, with an emphasis throughout on China. Apart from exhibitions, the museum also promotes a variety of educational activities and cultural events. It is the one museum which reflects the wider more complex world in which Bath is now located. Finally, the Bath Abbey Heritage Vaults are a good place to explore Bath's medieval history as a major monastic centre.

The Sporting City

Most people who connect Bath with sport at all would immediately think of rugby. It is very public, happening as it does on the Recreation Ground (the Rec) immediately across the river from the Grand Parade. With crowds of ten thousand, it can be very noisy in the centre of Bath on match days. Both before and after the game, the streets of Bath will be full of rugby supporters. Rugby is big business now, and shops, pubs and restaurants all benefit from the presence of Bath Rugby in the city centre. The Rec is a wonderful setting for any activity. Cyril Beazer, a local builder long associated with the club, quotes in his memoirs the view of one retired Battle of Britain pilot that "the bloody rugby is awful but it is worth coming to Bath just to sit in the stand and look at the view."

The high profile of Bath Rugby, both locally and nationally, makes it even more surprising that the club, so often league and cup winners at the highest level of the English game, is essentially homeless. The Rec was bequeathed to the care of the city fathers many years ago, with a covenant that makes it clear that it is to be used for a variety of recreational and sporting activities. Gradually the rugby club, the chief tenant of the Rec, has persuaded the trustees to allow it to develop a swanky clubhouse and to permit more and more temporary stands to boost the capacity to ten thousand. But the Charity Commission has so far refused to countenance the kind of major stadium that the club feels it needs to compete at the highest level of the now professional game. Many miles of news stories and Letters to the Editor have been written on this subject, which arouses heated and acrimonious debate in the city. Sponsorship of the "Keep Rugby at the Rec" campaign by the *Bath Chronicle* made it even more difficult to obtain impartial coverage of the issues surrounding the future of the Rec and the rugby club. At various times the club has threatened to leave the city altogether, and it is hard to predict how long the present stalemate can endure, or what will happen in the future.

Bath did well in the final years of the amateur era, under its inspirational coach Jack Rowell and with a number of truly outstanding local players including Jeremy Guscott. Despite European successes, the club has struggled to maintain its high ranking in the English rugby world. At various times, it has been racked by scandal, especially related to off-the-field activities of its stars such as heavy drinking and drug-taking. As other clubs made shrewd moves to enhance their grounds, move to new ones or come to ground-sharing arrangements with football clubs, Bath has begun to trail with its strictly limited ground capacity and the high level of energy devoted to simply remaining on the Rec and investigating alternatives.

It is interesting to contrast the dithering about its future with the decisive action taken by one junior side, the Stothert & Pitt Rugby Club. Unlike other parts of England, rugby in the Bath-Bristol area has roots beyond the private schools, and it is indicative that this famous old engineering firm had a rugby club before it had a football club. When the firm closed in the late 1980s (largely thanks to the devilish antics of Robert Maxwell who acquired ownership in that decade but was more interested in the pension fund than making cranes) the rugby club decided it would survive and thrive, and had soon arranged finance to purchase a new ground and build a clubhouse just off the A4 road at Saltford.

The fortunes of football in the city have followed a rather different course. Bath City Football Club has never been a League team, not for the want of trying. For many years it prided itself on being a leading non-league club, generally in the Southern League. The club also acquired a formidable reputation for victories against league teams in the FA Cup. For those used to seeing Chelsea or Manchester United on television, a visit to Twerton Park must be a shock. This is what football grounds used to look like: a gaunt, rather shabby stand to sit in, and along the entire length of one side a high covered terrace on which to stand. Where Bath Rugby close the gates on capacity 10,000 crowds, a gate of 1,000 is considered good at Twerton.

The very location of the club is significant. This is working-class, industrial Bath, where a majority of spectators still speak with local accents. It is a constant battle to hang on to both spectators and commercial sponsors. But there are many compensations: a friendly and comfortable bar and social club, neighbouring fields used by Bath City Farm, a stunning view of Beckford's Tower and Georgian Bath climbing the slopes of Lansdown, and that special sense of being part of something local and real. And crucially, unlike the rugby club, Bath City owns its ground. But for the moment, Bath is stuck in a time-warp: rugby on the Rec and football at Twerton, and little love lost between the two.

Bath City Football Club has seen off opposition from an unexpected quarter in recent years—Bath University. As we have seen, the university inherited some well maintained sports fields at Claverton Down. It built on this to become a major sports university, centred on a large and well equipped sports centre which includes a fifty-metre swimming pool. All their sporting activities operate under the heading of Team Bath. They combine the usual student sports activities with providing a base for amateur teams in sports such as hockey which compete at regional and national level. Over the years a large empire has grown at Claverton, and individual stars have come to national importance, most recently Amy Williams. Having won a gold medal at the 2010 Winter Olympics, she has since become the first woman to become an Honorary Freeman of the City of Bath.

The main controversy has been over the football team, where sports centre director Ged Roddy added to his academic role by managing a semi-professional football team, which allowed young footballers to mix academic study with their sport. Although for several seasons Team Bath and Bath City shared the ground at Twerton (and training facilities at the university) and were in the same league, this aroused strong feelings in the city. The accusation of "football on the taxes" surfaced and eventually the university was forced to admit that while their Department of Education grant was not used for this purpose, some of their discretionary income was certainly going that way. With Bath City struggling to survive on a large amount of voluntary effort, harsh words were said. At the end of the 2008/09 season the university withdrew its support and Team Bath resigned from the League.

The Festival City

Once there was a Bath Festival. Now there are Bath festivals. Dispersal has been a process that began gradually but which has accelerated in recent years as society itself becomes more diverse and the market for cultural activities more segmented between different interest groups. The Bath Festival was conceived in London, though it took some years to reach birth. The re-opening of the Assembly Rooms in Bath in 1937 had brought Bath to the attention of the London artistic circles. A meeting was called at the Royal Opera House in October 1938 to explore possibilities. There was a buzz of excitement but the war intervened. Post-war the idea of an arts festival in the city was revived, and the first Assembly, as it was then called, was held in 1948.

Since then it has been an annual early summer event every year with the exception of 1956 and 1957. Over the years, there has been much debate about the purpose of the festival. A *Bath Chronicle* leader on 1 June 1949 suggested that "the Assembly (festival) is very much part of the city's 'business' as the premier spa in Britain". There is no doubt that this desire to bring visitors and business to the city has been an important factor in driving the festival forward. But who should pay, and how much, to ensure that it happened? And within these generalized questions, there is a more specific one about the role and purpose of public subsidy of the arts, and even more specific questions about the contributions of the Arts Council, and of local authorities.

A factor that has continually held the festival back is the issue of venues, especially for classical music. The newly rebuilt Assembly Rooms were the main venue for chamber music, although their acoustics have been much criticized. (One critic suggested they might be turned into a swimming pool.) The Pavilion, abutting the Recreation Ground and Leisure Centre, has always been a barn of a building, probably more suited to all-in wrestling and pop concerts than classical orchestras. The Forum, at the bottom end of town, only became available when its life as a cinema was over. There were problems over the use of Bath Abbey, where the church refused to sanction applause, a problem that continued until the late 1980s. As late as 1987, Geoffrey Lester, rector of the abbey, stated that "the church is not a public place", a view that seemed at odds with the fact that it is one of the most visited buildings in the city. The Theatre Royal, pretty as it is, was felt to be a difficult space for both opera and recitals. Amelia Freedman, director in the late 1980s and early 1990s, liked St. George's Brandon Hill in Bristol as a venue for chamber music, as well as Bristol's Colston Hall and Wells Cathedral for major orchestral and choral works. But the spreading of the festival outside Bath has always raised hackles in the city. Even so, the years came and went, and there was no serious attempt to provide Bath with an international concert hall to match the international aspirations of its festival.

Historically, a high point of the festival was the decade of the 1960s with Yehudi Menuhin at the helm and "Menuhin and friends and family", as they were often referred to, doing much of the creative work. Criticism of the elitism of the festival was constant, not helped by Menuhin's fleeting visits to the city where he stayed in private suites at the Lansdown Grove Hotel. The festival "fringe" at this time referred to a series of social events aimed at the same well-off middle-class people who attended concerts, such as the infamous Roman Orgy of 1961 or the Cave Rave at Cheddar in 1962. But there were also some more popular events, such as the street dancing to jazz bands—called Jambeano—around the town, enough indeed to make Menuhin feel that his concept of an international classical music festival was being diluted. In 1968 Menuhin was sacked. He complained in the *Daily Telegraph* that "I wanted Bath eventually to become something like Tanglewood in Massachusetts with its own concert hall and providing something large for the region and particularly its youth. But this was not taken up, partly of course because of the silly jealousies between Bath and Bristol."

It was a very different man, much closer to the pulse of the 1960s and all that meant in creative England, who took the festival forward. Sir Michael Tippett, an internationally acclaimed composer, lived at nearby Corsham and was Bath Festival Director from 1969-74. Under his guidance the festival blossomed in many directions. In 1969 a Blues Festival on the Recreation Ground attracted 30,000 people and brought chaos to the city. It was not the sort of event that Bath was used to. At last the festival spawned a true fringe, in its early days called The Other Festival. Tippett visited and called it "a glorious jamboree, just what it ought to be". The times were certainly changing and the fringe included a Gay Liberation Ball.

In recent years, Bath Festival, now more clearly defined as the International Music Festival, has continued to enjoy a high and deserved reputation for presenting the very best in classical music and jazz, with innovative choices of music, artists and settings. Its concerts are often broadcast by BBC radio. My own outstanding memory is a performance by Jason Thornton and the Bath Philharmonia of Mahler's Eighth Symphony (the "Symphony of a Thousand") at Green Park Station in May 2000. It was not easy, there were other users of the old railway station such as market stall holders to be pacified. But Thornton was a man with a mission, having accepted a bet in 1995 to conduct all nine Mahler symphonies by the millennium. Eight down (mostly at the Forum), one to go, and this was, then, the climax. In addition to his orchestra, there was the Bath Millennium Festival Chorus, the London Philharmonic Chorus, Bournemouth Symphony Chorus and local school choirs from Hayesfield and Bath Royal High. It rained, as sometimes happens in Bath, but the audience, well over a thousand of us, arrived, settled ourselves and sat enthralled as Mahler's great tapestry was unrolled before us. Towards the end of the evening, the clouds fled away, there was late evening sunshine, and a blackbird began to sing on a tree just outside the station. Mahler would have loved it. Sitting towards the back, we could hear it so clearly; amazingly so could the conductor. Years later, the words blackbird and Mahler still conjured up for him one of the great nights of his musical career.

Bath Festivals is now the umbrella organization for three festivals: Bath International Music Festival in early summer, the Literature Festival in very early spring and the autumnal Children's Literature Festival. When Menuhin resigned, he referred to "the ills of the century and possible cures and solutions". In some ways, the Literature Festival has taken up this challenge. Every literature festival lives in constant danger of simply reproducing the tiresome sequence in which the author talks about the latest book, answers anodyne questions from the audience, the bookshop sells books, the author signs books and catches the next train to London. Yes, this happens, but other things happen too. I remember vividly a three-woman symposium on Daphne du Maurier followed by a screening of *Rebecca* at the Little Theatre which completely changed my view of that author.

The walks that have disappeared from the Music Festival programme have reappeared in the Literature Festival. In 2010 each day had a theme: Britain, Shakespeare, Food, Politics, Music, Minds, Bodies, Rome, France. There was scope for rubbing of shoulders between events, for an audience to take a broader view of a subject than they might get from one author, one book. Add in an excellent bookshop run by Bath's own Mr B's Emporium of Reading Delights, and even an old cynic like the present author can look forward to the Bath Literature Festival. The only improvement I might suggest to both this and the Children's Literature Festival is to invite rather more rising stars from the region and rather less fading stars from London.

There are other festivals in Bath too. When Amelia Freedman left as artistic director of the International Music Festival, she founded the Bath Mozart Fest, of which she remains the artistic director. This takes place in November, in those usually cold and dark days before the Bath Christmas Market brightens the lives of Bathonians and visitors alike. The Mozart Fest receives no public subsidy, existing entirely on ticket sales and sponsorship, a considerable achievement. Then there is the Film Festival—and the Folk Festival and Comedy, Banjo, Dance and Jane Austen Festivals. From time to time other festivals rise and fall. It is a competitive world, but it helps to fill hotel beds, pubs, restaurants, and hopefully brings a little pleasure to local people too.

The Bath Fringe Festival now begins at roughly the same time as the Music Festival but continues a week longer. It spreads over an amazing 35 sites in the city. Withdrawal of their local authority grant (except for visual arts) has made it impossible to support some of the larger outdoor events that have taken place in the past but even so it remains an impressive and very diverse programme of theatre, cabaret, circus, dance, comedy, music, spoken word and a group joyously described as unclassifiable. Arguably it is the stronger and fitter for not depending on local authority funding, especially as the country enters a period of drastic cuts in public expenditure.

Some of the most successful events in Bath are based in local communities within the city. One such is the annual Widcombe Rising. Now Widcombe can be an austere place. My earliest memories of it are looking across the river from Bath Spa station at the rooftop slogans of the Widcombe Baptist Church that variously warn us (still) that "Christ died for your sins" and "Prepare to Meet thy God". The effect is rather softened by a set of modern "community rooms" built around the austere cube of the original building, even more so on Widcombe Rising Day with hundreds of people sitting around on the grass outside, eating, drinking, chattering. Claverton Street is closed for the day and is lined with stalls and performers, spreading out into the lower parts of Widcombe Hill and Ralph Allen Drive. There are stages for the bands, a Big Wheel (the 'Widcombe Eye') for children large and small and a helter-skelter for child-sized children. It is the middle of June, the sun shines and no-one would argue with the organizers' claim that this is "Bath's biggest street party". At St. Matthew's Church the festivities are a little more decorous, with cream teas, a history exhibition about the canal and handbell ringing.

The old schoolroom (the Widcombe Institute) opposite the church is now home to the Natural Theatre Company, whose brainchild this is. Bath is fortunate indeed to have these internationally recognized exponents of street theatre in its midst. Formed in 1970, they now perform at worldwide events, including World Expo in Shanghai, Skyride in Manchester City Centre, the Melbourne Comedy Festival in Australia, the Barry Street Festival in Wales and in seafront entertainment in Cleethorpes. Originally, the Widcombe Rising was a kind of festive roads protest, since on every day except Widcombe Rising Day, Widcombe has to suffer the constant churning of traffic making its way round from the London Road and

Cleveland Bridge towards the Wells Road and Lower Bristol Road. It has grown from a protest into a way of life, and long may it continue.

St. Michael's Church

8 | **Faith in the City**
The Religious Landscape

"The Lord thy God bringeth thee into a good land, a land of brooks of water, of fountains and depths that spring out of valleys and hills."

Deuteronomy, 8, 7

Wise, compassionate, humble, Thomas Ken is widely regarded as one of the greatest of all those who have held the title of Bishop of Bath and Wells. He quoted the words above in the preface to a special prayer book he wrote for the use of those coming to take the waters in Bath, rich and poor alike, within a year of taking up his new position in 1684. He did not shrink from including prayers for the destitute whose poverty prevented them from taking advantage of the waters, just as he did not shrink in 1685 from attending to the physical and spiritual needs of the prisoners rounded up after the failure of the Monmouth Rebellion and imprisoned in his palace at Wells. He made clear links between religion and health, seeing illness as a trial for good people and a punishment for the bad. He urged those coming to Bath to pray thus:

> Ah, Lord, it is the cure of my soul for which I pray more earnestly than for the cure of my body. I go to the bath for my bodily health, and do Thou bless it, if it be Thy will, to my perfect recovery, and to the recovery of all those that come hither with me. But for the health of my soul I fly to the blood of Jesus. I consult my bodily physician for my distemper, but with much greater concern I fly to Thee, O Lord, who art the Sovereign Physician of Souls.

Within the parish of Widcombe is Holloway, and in Holloway is an old horse trough. Older people in the area remember well a poem about kindness to animals that used to be inscribed on the wall here. This steep and difficult hill was once the main entrance to Bath from the south. Now the horse trough has been tidied up and the poem is back, inscribed on a new plaque unveiled at a ceremony attended by the Natural Theatre Company's Lady Margaret and the Widcombe Mummers:

A man of kindness to his beast is kind,
For brutal actions show a brutal mind.
Remember! He who made thee, made the brute,
Who gave thee speech and reason, formed him mute.
He can't complain, but God's all-seeing eye
Beholds thy Cruelty and hears his cry.
He was designed thy Servant, not thy Drudge
Remember! His Creator is thy Judge.

In 1850 William Hurn, Bathonian, sailed off to a new life in South Australia. As a boy he had learned these words off by heart and was able to reproduce them much as here in a letter to a paper back home on animal welfare.

In earlier centuries, it was sick humans rather than suffering horses who received charity here, for opposite the horse trough is the Magdalen Chapel, the only vestige of a medieval lepers' hospital that once stood on this site. This steep north-facing slope of Beechen Cliff was damp and often sunless, but it did have fresh water from several springs. The hospital dated back to the twelfth century and was in the care of the Benedictine monks of Bath Abbey. By the seventeenth century the hospital was caring for the mentally ill rather than lepers and in 1761 was rebuilt. This house, now called Magdalen Cottage, can be seen a short way farther down the hill. But the chapel itself did not thrive: visitors carried off much of the fifteenth-century stained glass (at least, that is the story), and most of the congregation left when St. Mark's Church was opened down in Widcombe during the religious revival of the 1830s.

Remarkably, while St. Mark's has been transformed into a busy community centre, Magdalen Chapel has survived. It survived bombing during the Second World War and the "Sack of Bath" destruction of lower Holloway and such familiar landmarks as the Young Fox pub and the much-loved "Dolls' Hospital" run by Leslie Law, the "Dr. Kildare of Holloway". Now it is home to a small but lively congregation that loves music, and has established its own Festival Week (another festival) of concerts that take place every July. It is no mean achievement in one of the smallest churches in Bath. After morning service on fine days, the congregation takes coffee in the garden, with fine views over the city framed by two walnut trees which still produce a good crop of nuts. It is a good place to restore one's faith in the city

Bishop Ken's prayer-book, the lepers' hospital, the Holloway horse trough and the Magdalen Chapel are all useful reminders that "Faith in the City" can refer to two related sets of ideas. It implies fairly obviously the past and current state of religious belief in the city and how that is organized. But it also implies a certain belief that a well-run city is a creation of culture and civilization. Is there more to the city than organising ever more opportunities for shopping or for over-indulgence? I believe there is, and that churches, chapels and religious organizations have made a major contribution over the years to making the city a better, more compassionate place in which to live. Nowadays we find them engaged not just in religious observance, but in youth work, in staging concerts, mounting exhibitions, providing venues for meetings for many voluntary organizations, activity clubs for older people, holiday play schemes—the list is endless. Not to mention helping individuals and families to mark the rituals of birth, marriage and death. This city, any city, would be a poorer place without them.

Respectable Congregations and Non-Conformists

Belief of course did not begin with the Christians. From the garden of the Magdalen Chapel, Bath Abbey stands etched against, on the horizon, the flat profile of Solsbury Hill camp where our pre-Roman ancestors no doubt worshipped their own gods in their own ways. They tried to understand the movement of the stars, to come to terms with the cycle of birth and death and the mystery of the seasons. We have seen too how the Romans appropriated the older belief systems to their own pantheon of gods, and how they fell into the thrall of the newly minted Christian explanation of things. Now in Bath there are people belonging to many different Christian denominations, people of no clear belief system at all, and also believers in other faiths such as Islam, Judaism or Buddhism. There are once again Pagans in Bath too.

Perhaps it is time to return to the eighteenth century, when some people at least knew their place. Bath had a problem: fashionable people, people of wealth and rank were swarming to the city. On Sundays they wanted to go to church. Not all could be fitted into existing churches, and in any case they would not want to mix with ordinary people attending those churches. If the problem seems an artificial one to modern eyes, the solution was even more extraordinary. Four private chapels, functioning like small businesses, sprang up around the city. The Octagon Chapel in Milsom Street, always the most fashionable of Bath's shopping streets, has already been mentioned in relation to William Herschel, the astronomer who began his Bath career as the organist here, and also as the temporary home during the twentieth century of the Royal Photographic Society. It remained a chapel until 1895, and is the only one of these four chapels to have survived intact, although it faces an uncertain future.

Funds were raised by subscription and the enterprise was promoted by a banker. Essentially this is an octagon fitted into a square room, with a gallery above supported by Ionic columns, and lit by an elegant lantern. It opens through a corridor into Milsom Street, and externally there is no indication of such a lovely building behind. During a recent Bath Literature Festival, it was pressed into service as a concert recital hall for a young and gifted virtuoso violinist, Ruth Palmer. A slim figure in black in the centre of this extraordinary space, Ruth captivated a full house with her rendition of a Bach Partita for solo violin and a Bartok Sonata. Both performer and audience seemed delighted by the perfect acoustics. No wonder Herschel liked it. At the inauguration of the organ in 1767, Handel's *Messiah* was performed and one imagines that the society figures who attended the chapel were just as impressed by the quality of the music as by the fervour of the preachers.

There is less to be seen and less to be said about the other chapels. The first of these was St. Mary's in Chapel Row, promoted by John Wood the Elder and a consortium of residents. Designed by Wood himself, it is supposed to have been a lovely little classical temple. Unfortunately it was demolished in 1875 to improve access to the new Midland Railway station at Green Park from Queen Square. A small relic of it can be spotted lurking in some nondescript bushes.

Margaret Chapel, hidden behind houses in Brock Street and the little pedestrian shopping alley of Margaret's Buildings, must have been a real curiosity. Like the Countess of Huntingdon Chapel it was built (in 1773/4) in the gothic style by none other than Wood the Younger, fresh from the heavy classical grandeur of the Royal Crescent. The chapel was declared redundant when the vast church of St. Andrew was opened behind the Royal Crescent. The last of the four private chapels was the Laura Chapel which served the growing estate of Bathwick across the river. The entrances can still be seen in Henrietta Street, clearly marked, but alas where the chapel was once there is now a row of garages. Well heated, sweet-smelling and directed by smooth-talking clerics, these chapels both served the narrow religious sentiments of eighteenth-century Bath and marked their inadequacies.

Not all Christians were prepared to accept uncritically the den of iniquity that Bath was widely considered to be in the mid-eighteenth century. The early Methodist leaders George Whitfield and John Wesley were frequent visitors to preach what they saw as the Word of God to the many who were excluded from the existing Anglican churches where most pews were purchased and owned by respectable families. The central figure and benefactor of the early evangelical movement was Selina, Countess of Huntingdon, who had inherited a large fortune based on coal-mines in the Midlands and North of England. Not only were the early Methodists supported by her, but also the Moravians who were active in Bath from the middle of the eighteenth century. She managed the apparently impossible—to be both a successful society lady and an active critic of many of that society's vices: gambling, over-indulgence in food and alcohol, adultery. Edith Sitwell devotes a whole chapter to the countess in her book on Bath, and concludes that in her life "piety and worldly wisdom were present in equal proportions". Her gothic chapel in the Vineyards became an integral part of Bath life, a place where fashionable society could confront its own shortcomings. Lady Buckingham complained that "It is monstrous to be told that you have a heart as sinful as the common wretches of the earth."

Yet it was the public preaching of Wesley which in the long run was to have a greater impact on English society. He also left his mark in Bath. Kingswood School on Lansdown, now a private, fee-paying school, began life with Wesley's evangelical work among the coal-miners of Kingswood, just north of Bristol. Wesley preached at the chapel in the Vineyards, and Horace Walpole left a detailed note of the event, mentioning even an element of comfort for the "elect ladies" in the balcony, by contrast with the wooden benches in the rest of the chapel.

Religious groups are always under pressure to respond to social change. In the eighteenth century, as Bath grew very rapidly, there was a shortage of church places, especially outside the old bound-aries of the city wall, and in Walcot especially. The non-conformist groups were meanwhile gathering in strength and importance. One of the loveliest churches in the city, St. Swithin's at Walcot, represents a more substantial response by the established Church to the city's sudden expansion than the private chapels, but still serving a quite narrow sector of society. To be accurate, this is not a new church. In 1740 it was decided to rebuild the tiny village church: John Wood the Elder produced a design, as did Robert Smith, a churchwarden. Smith's gothic design was chosen and Wood refused ever to enter the church again. It was a snub to the man who was attempting to impose on Bath the new architectural language of classicism exem-plified in Queen Square.

Within thirty years the building had clearly not kept up with the Bath boom, and it was again rebuilt, this time to a neoclassical design by John Palmer, the city architect. At this point it had an open layout much as we see today after a recent refurbishment, a design well suited to today's evangelical forms of worship. The end two bays added in 1788 turned the church from a square into an oblong, and in 1792 Smith's tower was replaced by the present elegant spire.

St Swithin's was a fashionable church for residents and visitors alike. There are many, many connections. Jane Austen's parents were married here in Smith's church, and George, her father, was buried here. There is a memorial plaque in the garden. Another plaque remembers Fanny Burney, the novelist. One of the many memorials lining the church walls is in memory of her husband, General Alexandre d'Arblay, who had fled the Terror in France following the Revolution. Sadly there is no note in the church to celebrate the fact that William Wilberforce, campaigner for the abolition of the slave trade, was married here in 1797. The couple spent their honeymoon inspecting Hannah More's Sunday schools in rural Somerset. One other man not remembered in the church but buried in the little graveyard on the other side of Walcot Street is "Citizen" John Thelwall. Friend of Coleridge and Dorothy and William Wordsworth and a political radical of the 1790s, he reinvented himself in the new century as a lecturer on public speaking and the founder of speech therapy. He died while on a lecture tour to Bath.

St. Swithin's did not solve the problem of insufficient church places in the parish of Walcot. In the eighteenth century pew rents were a major source of income for the Church of England, with perhaps a few benches provided for the poor. Another church, Christchurch in Julian Road, was opened in 1798, and this time did provide 800 free places with a further 400 rented places in the galleries. But many parishioners had long given up the established Church in favour of the now confident and outward-looking non-conformist groups in the city. Walcot Methodist Church, Manvers Street Baptist Church and the Argyle Chapel (United Reformed Church) are three fine buildings that continue to exemplify the power and influence of non-conformity in Bath.

At the other end of Walcot Street from St. Swithin's is another of Bath's best known churches, St. Michael's—or to give its full title, St. Michael's Without. It is indeed outside the old city bound-aries, although to modern eyes a church in view of the abbey, at a busy traffic intersection and opposite the new build of the Podium shopping centre, library and car-park, looks very urban indeed. It is a busy and ambitious place, as its website makes clear: "We aspire to be a serving, loving, engaging, inspiring, hospitable, honest, praying and worshipping group of people." St. Michael's works closely with the Genesis Trust, a local Christian organization with a wide remit to work with people who are homeless or just plain poor (more of this in Chapter 11). The particular contribution of St. Michael's is the twice weekly Lunch Box project, which provides cheap meals in the crypt for those who are homeless or on low incomes.

The boldest gesture that St. Michael's has taken is to replace the pews with comfortable, modern seating. This is ideal for talks and concerts as well as church services. It also allows the equally bold move of using the church as a café during weekdays, which has proved popular with locals and tourists alike. With its bright, airy Victorian interior, it makes a welcome addition to the range of city centre cafés and is also a fund-raiser for the ASHA project in the slums of Delhi, India. This supports individuals and communities through education, health, providing sanitation and fresh water. This corner where Broad Street, Walcot Street and Northgate Street meet is arguably the busiest in the city, and the church represents something calmer, slower, more enduring, more committed to that civilizing mission of the city.

In the eighteenth and nineteenth centuries Christian churches were springing up all over the place. Their story in twentieth-century Bath is rather a tale of destruction, closures and amalgamations. Most of the damage was done during the Second World War by air-raids. In the more secular world of post-1945, almost as if so much destruction had turned people away from organized religion, rebuilding churches was not seen as a high priority. Churches which had been only slightly damaged, such as the Magdalen Chapel and the abbey (to take the smallest and biggest), were repaired. But a number of very large churches, notably St. Andrew's in Julian Road, disappeared. Nowadays visitors take the smooth outline of the Royal Crescent for granted. Yet for eighty years it was dominated by the giant tower of Sir Gilbert Scott's church built on a piece of land behind the Royal Crescent Mews. The tower survived the bombing, the church did not (Pevsner, blunt as ever, said it was "happily bombed"), and the tower in its turn was taken down (Pevsner: "a blessing"). Now there is a triangle of grass and opposite a small, rather ugly replacement for St. Andrew's. Now that too is shut, although the building still serves as a hall for the school next door, a dual use envisaged right from the start. The congregation has moved to St. Swithin's in the same parish of Walcot.

Closer to the city centre is St James' Parade and James Street West, but where is St. James' Church? The church had stood at the bottom of Stall Street since medieval times. John Palmer had rebuilt it in the eighteenth century and an Italianate tower had been added in the nineteenth. By 1945 only the walls and tower remained. In 1957 the whole lot came down, for this is shopping Bath and the interests of Woolworths and Marks & Spencer prevailed over possible rebuilding or even (as at the old Coventry Cathedral) retention as a war memorial.

The most curious tale is that of the severely bombed Holy Trinity church near Green Park Station, the remains of which were also removed in 1957. This had been paid for in the 1820s by the Church Building Commission, the body empowered by Parliament to make good the woeful lack of Anglican churches in the country, especially those providing free places for the urban poor. The congregation, adherents of a ceremonial Catholic form of worship within the Church of England, were then invited to use the nearby St. Paul's Church Hall in Monmouth Place. When the vicar of St. Paul's retired in 1952, the congregation then moved into St. Paul's Church in Monmouth Street, which thus became Holy Trinity. The full story is bizarre and complex to those not immersed in the obscure religious politics of the Church of England, and includes a popular priest who "went over" to the Church of Rome. All is revealed on the website of Holy Trinity church.

Weston: the Christian Mission in the Twenty-First Century

It is impossible to name all the Christian churches and sects in Bath, and perhaps more useful to focus on a much smaller area. Curiously, both the sects encouraged by the Countess of Huntingdon—her Connexion and the Moravians—are present in Weston despite the fact that to the casual eye, the suburban village continues to cluster around its Church of England church. Organized religion has always been hard-going in Weston: remember those washerwomen who thought there were much more exciting things to be done on Sunday than go to church. In the second half of the twentieth century there has been much new housing here, initially mostly council accommodation, but more recently a lot of private housing too, and Weston has its share of social problems. What the church had was space, a parish hall and the old Church of England primary school as well. The response of the church in Weston has been to refurbish the nineteenth-century school house as All Saints' Centre, formally opened in 2001 by Jim Thompson, Bishop of Bath and Wells. "Bishop Jim" was known for his frequent appearances on Radio 4's morning *Thought for the Day*, his outspoken social and political views and especially his open criticism of the poverty and social upheavals caused by Margaret Thatcher's government when he was Bishop of Stepney in London's East End.

All Saints' Centre provides more than just a social service. It is the headquarters of More to Life, a joint church initiative to encourage community events in Weston and Newbridge. The centre advertises spaces for conferences, seminars, training, weddings and parties. It is businesslike and efficient. On an August afternoon when the church was shut and the vicar on holiday, the office was determinedly open. Downstairs, there was a gentle exercise class for older women in full swing. Next door, the village nursery was busy doing what nurseries do best—playing—in what had once been an overcrowded and dingy school. The church also employs both a childworker and a youth worker, and there are regular concerts and on Sundays, church services too.

The Countess of Huntingdon Connexion Chapel is in Trafalgar

Road, just off the High Street, a little gothic stone chapel fitting in well with its stone-built neighbours. Down the slope is the handsome pre-Georgian King's Head pub (one of three still open in the village) and opposite the chapel are equally handsome stone houses. Uphill, the green fields of Lansdown can be seen. Until it closed its doors in July 2010, the chapel was a lively place with its own pastor, and still advertised youth, ladies, and prayer evenings. There are still flowers—fuchsias and roses—at the gate. It is curious that a sect that spread to the United States of America, and through returning freed slaves to Sierra Leone in West Africa, should have maintained a chapel for so many years so close to the mother chapel in Bath.

The main non-conformist option in the village now, though, is the Moravian Church at the far end of the High Street. Externally, there is little to be said in favour of this building which is definitely of its time, the 1950s. The Moravians have been in Bath a long time. Led by John Cennick, a great preacher, they came from Kingswood, just north of Bristol, where John Wesley was also active preaching to the coal-miners in the early days of Methodism. By 1765 they had a congregation in Monmouth Street. But over their first hundred years in Bath, their evangelical fervour seems to have diminished, and in 1845 they moved to an elaborate neoclassical building in Charlotte Street designed by John Wilson. It is still there, and after some years as a Christian Scientist church it has found a new use as rather grand offices. In 1907 the Moravians joined the move out to the new suburbs, in their case Coronation Avenue in Oldfield Park, a respectable working-class community of stone terraces where other non-conformist sects were already established.

Roll the clock forward another fifty years, and the Moravians were back in missionary mode once more. Following discussion by the non-conformist Free Church Council in Bath, the Moravians were given responsibility for Weston, where their target was the new council housing developments. As a plaque in the church records, the finance was provided by insurance money from Moravian premises in Fetters Lane, London, bombed out in the Blitz.

Moravians like to live out their mission in every aspect of their lives, and their role in the village is to provide facilities, meeting-places, social contact in a privatised stay-at-home society. They encourage healthier, more satisfying lifestyles: badminton, the Boys' Brigade, children's music-making, Guides, a lunch club for the elderly, a model railway club, the Townswomen's Guild, Kung Fu, a women's group. It sounds much like the All Saints' Centre but maybe a little more down market, easily affordable, in the words of the minister, Beth Torkington, who is not just a minister but a bishop too, spending half her time in Weston and the other half of her time in a wider leadership role within the church. She is slightly bemused, perhaps even amused, by the goings-on in the Anglican Church over women bishops. The Moravian Church has a strong record on encouraging women, and once they started to become ministers, it was accepted that they would become bishops too. She is the third within the Moravian Church, but the first in Europe. On current trends, the Moravian Church, any church, will die out soon, she says. She does not believe that will happen, and in the meantime, the Moravians continue their mission of working alongside the people.

Catholic Bath

No doubt the Roman Catholics would be shocked at any thought of dying out. In Bath terms they appear rather belatedly on the scene. The post-Reformation history of Catholicism in Bath, after Henry VIII had broken the links between the English Church and Rome, begins at Bell Tree House on the corner of Stall Street and what is now Beau Street (then called Bell Tree Lane). It had been the Parsonage House for St. James' Church in Stall Street, and when St. James' passed to the Bath Corporation, Mr. Hussey of Marnhull, Dorset, bought it as a meeting place for Catholics. Despite the fact that it was used as such by several of the Gunpowder Plotters in 1605 this arrangement continued much without incident until the eighteenth century, when a new chapel was built between St. James' Parade and Lower Borough Walls. The newly built (or renovated— the evidence is unclear) chapel and houses were burned down by the anti-Catholic Gordon rioters in 1780. (Mild enough compared to London, but the authorities executed one of the mob to allay the fears of visitors to the city that such an event might be repeated.)

Some visitors simply packed their bags and fled, including Fanny Burney. The evidence on the ground is confusing: there is indeed a gap in St. James' Parade and a small open green space which used to be a burial ground, but the Chapel Arts Centre here is so called not because of the Roman Catholic chapel but because it occupies the St James' Memorial Hall, built a full century later.

Despite this setback, Roman Catholic numbers were growing in Bath. When the new Theatre Royal opened in 1805, they seized the day and moved into the old theatre in Orchard Street. The floor was levelled and the galleries removed. At first burials took place in lead coffins in the damp basement, and the visitor can still see some, though most were removed to the Roman Catholic cemetery at Perrymead in the 1850s. This period of Catholic history in Bath is always associated with the redoubtable Bishop Baines. He arrived in Bath in 1817 and from 1823 until his death in 1843 he preached, argued and generally stirred up the religious life of the area, from 1829 as Vicar Apostolic of the Western District. Catholic Emancipation occurred in 1829 and Bishop Baines took full advantage to push a cautious and defensive and sometimes unwilling church towards the mainstream of English Christian life. His preaching style was so much admired that congregations numbered up to one thousand, and usually included a sprinkling of Protestants. He purchased Prior Park as a Catholic seminary, and it has continued to be a major Catholic fee-paying school ever since.

By the 1860s the Catholics of Bath were confident and wealthy enough to build the church of St. John the Evangelist at South Parade, its spire towering over the city from every viewpoint. Yet this was by no means the end of Roman Catholic building in the city. This brings us to solid, respectable, working-class Oldfield Park, where in the shadow of the old Somerset and Dorset Railway, and next door to the Wansdyke Business Centre and the old Co-op Dairy, is St. Alphege's Church. Designed by Sir Giles Gilbert Scott in the 1920s, it a small Roman basilica in an unlikely setting. Scott, better known for his vast Anglican cathedral in Liverpool, had already worked in Somerset at the Benedictine monastery of Downside. He was a young man, but even in later life he still liked his Bath church and wrote that "it has always been one of my favourite works". St. Alphege has a good local pedigree, having lived for some time as a solitary hermit on Lansdown, where a fresh water spring still bears his name. Within living memory the congregation in Oldfield Park would fetch water from the spring for their holy water stoop. They also plan to celebrate their hermit saint's centenary in 2012.

No doubt inspired by the rough exterior walls of St. John the Evangelist, Scott used rough Bath stone both externally and internally. He reflected that "Bath stone is usually used in an uninteresting way with regular courses having a smooth face; at St. Alphege's I have used stones that came out of the quarry in rough shapes and needed little more treatment than knocking off the greater projections." Such was, of course, the way of building in pre-Georgian times and many examples can be seen in the small towns and villages around Bath. Candlemas, which celebrates the presentation of Jesus, the light of the world, in the Temple in Jerusalem, is an important occasion here. To the accompaniment of Gregorian chant, one hundred people process round the church carrying lit candles, the flickering lights reflecting from every angle of the rough hewn surfaces. The light effects are exactly those of a mid-summer's evening in front of the Royal Crescent—only better, for this is a dark night in mid-winter in down-to-earth Oldfield Park.

City of the Dead: Cemeteries

The cruel description of Bath as a city of the dead and dying is probably exaggerated and out-of-date, but nevertheless the city has a great many cemeteries. At Combe Down, right by the old city boundary, next to the Foresters Arms pub and opposite where the Admiralty set up one of its hutted encampments during the Second World War (it is still there—for the moment), is Bath's Jewish cemetery. It contains fifty tombstones dating from between 1836 and 1921. They are modest, since unlike many English cities Bath has never had distinguished Jewish residents. Most inscriptions are in English and Hebrew, though a few are in Hebrew alone. It is surrounded by a seven-foot stone wall and contains a prayer room. An organization called the Friends of the Bath Jewish Burial Ground hopes to find the money to put the cemetery back into decent order.

Another special place among the cemeteries of Bath is the Quaker graveyard in Widcombe. There is a little flight of slippery steps at the end of Widcombe Terrace, a short road leading nowhere in particular, and a wooden door in a stone wall, framed by holly. You will need to know the code to get inside, but Bath Quakers are friendly and it is not too closely guarded a secret. The stone markers have been cleared and lie mainly against the walls. Jacob the tortoise lives here, his winter home in what appears to be an old coal-scuttle. He is fifty years old and wears a protective extra fibre glass shell after an accident to his own. The lowliest Quaker is as great as the richest and best-known Quaker, in life, in death, but I would want to single out two of the Friends remembered here: Robin and Heather Tanner. Robin was a school inspector and engraver and vastly influential in the enrichment of the post-Second World War primary school curriculum in the Bath area with all sorts of arts and crafts, and the development of the Crafts Study Centre at the Holburne Museum. In *Wiltshire Village*, his wife Heather wrote, beautifully, about the disappearing rural way of life, while Robin wrote about their entwined lives in *Double Harness*. Both books can be recommended to those who believe in a slower, richer way of life.

But of course there was a grander, more public, noisier way of life, and the great and the good are remembered as much in Bath as anywhere. Indeed, almost certainly more so, since so many came to live and die here. In particular, many retired colonial officers and military men retired to Bath. In Bath Abbey they have moved the memorials to the wall, and the assembled ranks are like so many calling cards from a bygone age. In 1844 a new cemetery was opened on the other side of Ralph Allen Drive, designed by the landscape architect John Claudius Loudon. He wanted the dead disposed of hygienically amid a rich botanical setting. Now the cemetery is wonderfully overgrown and collapsing in upon itself as all cemeteries should. It is a haven for wildlife and wild flowers, with minimal disturbance from the Council Parks Department. Nearby and equally attractive in a macabre way are the Smallcombe Cemetery (on the

National Trust Bath Skyline trail) and the Perrymead Roman Catholic cemetery. The latter is in well-named Pope's Walk, though I suspect the poet rather than the Bishop of Rome.

Currently most Bathonians are buried or cremated at the Council cemetery at Haycombe, next to Twerton Round Hill. It is crowded and busy, a friendly place, I have always thought, to lie. It commands a lovely view of the countryside south of Bath and the little village of Englishcombe. Those who care about such things will spot the remains of a medieval castle below them. It is a good place to sit and contemplate the future.

Christianity and Islam

The future is precisely what worries at least some of Bath's Christians. There are closures, there is joint use of one church by several de-nominations, there are dwindling congregations. Even the busy Quakers are reluctantly considering whether to leave their grand home in York Street, which had begun life as a Masonic Hall. It is a lovely building, but as the Bath Quakers' website insists: "Quaker Meetings can be held anywhere, and do not depend on there being a building of a particular shape, size or type." Yes, but... it must be worrying to committed Christians that fewer and fewer people want to participate in their collective acts of worship. Even the traditional association of the churches with births (christenings), marriages and deaths (funerals) seems almost to count against them. Church is alright for these "special" moments of extreme emotion, but for every Sunday, let alone every week day? Yet other aspects of the churches' work do seem to be wanted and appreciated. I was repeatedly told, during my enquiries into the world of Bath churches, about the im-portance of the churches' social mission. Work with the homeless, youth work with children, care for the elderly—all of these kept re-curring.

Such doubts and uncertainties were less apparent in Bath's Muslim community. Their issue about premises was not about en-couraging its use by other groups but the inadequacies of the present building for those wanting to use it. The Bath Islamic Society is a re-markable group. Many Islamic groups in England reflect the national and ethnic background of the majority of their members (e.g. Bengali, Somali, Pakistani) but the Bath Islamic Society attempts to support all Muslims regardless of their origins. The most obvious support is providing the Al Muzaffar mosque for prayer, in the basement of a house in Pierrepoint Street (the offices are above). There are also educational classes—a Saturday supplementary school for Muslim children and classes in English and IT for women. In addition, students from local schools visit the mosque as part of the religious education curriculum.

The Society would like to build its own mosque, but as Rashad Azami, the imam, explained, "nothing is in our favour". Firstly there is the obvious difficulty of finding a suitable site in Bath, and obtaining planning permission. Secondly there is the general climate in which, post-9/11, Islam and terrorism have become closely associated in the minds of people fed a constant stream of bad news and misinformation. Meanwhile they manage in their rather cramped conditions, with the help of a marquee in the back garden for special occasions. There are probably some 1,500 Muslims in Bath, most resident but some students at the college and universities, and some 350 attend the two congregations meeting for Friday prayers.

Certainly, the Bath Islamic Society works hard to get its message across. Weekly open days are held on Saturday and it maintains good relations with councillors, the local MP and other faiths. The Society attempts to meet head on the accusation that Islam is somehow "incompatible with English values", a charge which the imam rejects. He is an active member of the Bath Interfaith Group, and the festival of Eid, marking the end of the Ramadan month of fasting, is celebrated with a big party for both Muslims and non-Muslims at the Pavilion, one of the largest halls in the city. Yet even this has a rather controversial history. When it was first proposed that Muslims should take part in the Mayor's Call to Prayer, an annual event in the city, objections were raised by several Christian groups. It occasioned a large number of anti-Muslim letters to the local press. The compromise of having one event for the Christian community and a second event on an inter-faith basis seems less than satisfactory, but underlines the extent to which the Christian churches remain the accepted norm from which other faiths are seen as diverging. I suspect this is a decision which may have to be revisited in future years.

Emperor Haile Selassie, resident of Bath, 1936-41

9 | Changing Faces
Migration and Social Change

I n St. Swithin's Church are a great number of memorials to the "great and good" who thronged Georgian and Regency Bath. There is Robert Gardiner, who had spent "31 years in the Civil Service of the Honourable East India Company". There is Francis Russell, "born in Edinburgh of a virtuous and distinguished family. He passed the prime of life at Dacca in Bengal, the latter years of it in this city." The Museum of East Asian Art has a Chinese porcelain plate showing the arms of the Holburne of Menstrie family. Its central scene is Fort St. George in Madras, a major outpost of the East India Company. At St. Swithin's, colonial connections are not just with the East Indies but with the West Indies too. We find "Anne, relict of Walter Nisbet, of the island of Nevis, and daughter of Robert Parry of Llandrhaiadre [Llanrhaeadr], county of Denbigh." Many memorials are of military men, such as Sir Edward Berry, "friend and companion of Lord Nelson" and who fought alongside him at naval battles such as The Nile and Trafalgar. It is almost a relief to find on the balcony a memorial to someone as local as John Palmer, City Architect and also of course architect of St. Swithin's— one man who spent his working life in the city rather than building or defending the British Empire.

Georgian and Regency Bath was not a local city with a fixed population. Very many of its inhabitants came from elsewhere in the country, seeking a pleasant and fashionable place to visit and, in some cases, to settle. Going back in time from the eighteenth century, however, it would be reasonable to suppose that Bath was a much more local place, where most people were born, lived, worked and died. But even here there would be exceptions, especially among those fortunate enough to receive education and advancement through the Church. As we shall see in chapter 10, the life of Adelard of Bath (c.1080-c.1160), often described as "the first English scientist", is a good example of a man whose life was far from circumscribed by the circle of green hills within which Bath nestled.

Servants and Workers

The Bath of St. Swithin's and Georgian times required labour as it grew. The incomers to the city at this time were mostly wealthy people whose lifestyle created jobs: chairmen to carry them to and from the Baths, shop assistants to attend to their every whim and fancy, building craftsmen during the various booms in the building trade, laundry women to wash and iron their dirty clothes and linen. This was a consumer society before the term had been invented, and like our own twenty-first-century consumer society created a large number of poorly paid, low skill jobs in the service sector. According to local historian John Wroughton, during the 1830s one third of all Bath workers were in the domestic sector—mainly servants, but also gardeners, cooks and footmen. Wroughton points out that most of them "lived or lodged in Walcot", the rapidly growing suburb to the north-east of the city centre.

While many Bath workers lived relatively secure, if hard, lives, others were only employed during "the season" (i.e. in winter) and would go off in search of seasonal employment in agriculture in the summer. There was often hardship, too, among building workers when bad winter weather made work impossible, or during a slump in construction such as occurred in the early 1790s with consequent unemployment. Temporary work was often found for these unemployed men as a last resort, since Bath as a tourist city could hardly afford trouble (witness the efforts of the chairmen to quell anti-Catholic demonstrations at the time of the 1780 Gordon riots).

Nevertheless, the combination of a relatively stable economy based around services and concern on the part of the city fathers for the welfare of workers made Bath a particular focus for migrant labour. Conditions on the land were bad, and getting worse. When the Corn Laws were repealed, prices fell and wages too. By the 1870s, with cheap imports from Canada, agriculture was facing ruin. My own great-grandfather moved to Bath in the mid-century from the village of Chewton Mendip, high on the Mendip Hills, to the slums of Avon Street.

Bath continued to be a target for such inward migration into the twentieth century. Major employers such as Stothert & Pitt and the Horstmann Gear Company grew rapidly in size, and the labour market became less dependent on tourism and domestic service, although the latter continued to be the largest employer of women into the 1930s. New suburbs such as Oldfield Park grew to house the respectable working class whose wages had risen comfortably above the subsistence level. Many of them worshipped at the rather grand new non-conformist churches in the area, or in the new Roman Catholic church here too. Bath was becoming more spread out, more diverse, than before. By 1940, we can say with some confidence that Bath was on its way to becoming just another twentieth-century English town, just as it had once been just another Cotswold market-town. Of course, smoke-blackened and crumbling and largely ignored by the outside world, the Georgian masterworks were still there. But Bath had a life now beyond the Royal Crescent and the Circus. In the late 1930s, in recognition of the difficulties facing Bath's Georgian heritage, the decision was taken to restore the Assembly Rooms, which had been moonlighting as a cinema. It proved to be a rash decision. The new Assembly Rooms did not last long, destroyed by enemy bombs in 1941—as were many, many houses. One of the saddest memorials in St Swithin's is to the 39 civilians, including the rector, who were killed during the Second World War.

In addition to finding houses for those displaced by the Bath Blitz, the city had also to face the challenge of housing the many Admiralty staff transferred down from London. No doubt this was originally seen as a temporary measure, but the Admiralty liked Bath and stayed. It became a major employer in the city, rivalling Stothert & Pitt the crane-makers. It provided jobs both for those growing up in the city and civil servants transferring in from outside. The growth of the city continued apace, including the many decent peripheral estates, but also less happy redevelopment such as the Snow Hill flats off the London Road, and the streets north of Julian Road. In both cases, the houses destroyed were mostly solid, working-class houses of the Georgian and Regency periods. Many had fallen into disrepair, yet these were the houses that provided the essential context for the better-known showpieces of the Circus, squares and crescents.

But for most ordinary Bathonians, it was not the "Sack of Bath" in the 1970s so much as the "Sack of Britain" in the 1980s that created problems. I refer, of course, to the economic and social upheaval we once blamed on Margaret Thatcher, and eventually learned to call globalization. Capital would flow to places where labour was cheap and away from those where labour was dear; labour in Britain was not cheap, thanks in no small order to the work of the trade unions: therefore capital, and with it jobs, deserted Britain. The main casualty in Bath was Stothert & Pitt, bought up, asset stripped and closed down by Robert Maxwell. There was, even so, some growth in other forms of employment—higher education, the so-called "creative industries" such as publishing—and for these Bath, with all its seductive charms, was regarded as an ideal location. Put together with the sale of council houses, the failure to build new council housing and a wildly inflated property market that made Bath one of the most expensive places to live in the country, there were the conditions for a spectacular shift in population. Unable to buy or rent in Bath, many of the children of the council estates were forced to decamp to Peasedown, Radstock, Chippenham and Bristol. In their place, a new, wealthier, more vocal population has moved into the city, whether to work or to retire into the glories of the World Heritage City. Not to mention the students who now constitute about one in five of the total population of the city. Two universities in a city of less than 100,000 people is a considerable burden.

One of the ways in which I measure this great population shift is the rarity with which one hears "Bath" (or is it Barth, or Barf?) spoken in the city centre. That curious accent which is not Somerset, not Gloucestershire, not Wiltshire, not, least of all, Bristol (or is it Brissle?). That was the language that most of us (a few Admiralty types excepted) spoke at school. Now to find it, you may well have to take a bus out to Twerton or Fairfield Park or Odd Down. In such places Barf is alive and kicking, and I am assured still recognized as a language in the city's schools.

Another measure is the reluctance of these new Bathonians to observe the country courtesy of passing the time of day with complete strangers when out walking or waiting at a bus-stop. A third is the undeniable fact that those most likely to write to the local papers, sign petitions or attend protest meetings when someone suggests putting up a smart new modern building in the World Heritage City, are those relative newcomers. Some of them at least are prepared to acknowledge this. Indeed, those responsible for the UNESCO World Heritage tag are concerned that not all the people of Bath, especially the suburban working class, identify with or feel in any way affected by the world status of the city. This matters because it is, of course, the whole city, not just its Georgian buildings, which was awarded World Heritage status. It is a cleft stick the city's leaders are still trying to squeeze out of, and we shall leave them squirming for a little longer, before returning very briefly to Bath's future in Chapter 11.

Multicultural History

The obvious reason why this movement of people into and away from Bath has aroused little comment is that, unlike inward migration from Africa or Asia, it has involved mainly white people. The presence of black people in Bath, and the reasons for their presence is a complex story, and only the bare bones can be covered in this book. There are the noises, for example, that Matthew Bramble encounters in his first unsatisfactory lodgings in Bath in Smollett's *Humphrey Clinker*. There are "Two negroes, belonging to a Creole gentleman" practising the French horn—apparently gentlemen would regularly engage such musicians to announce them on social calls. These black men may be servants; equally they may be slaves, and it is one of the few literary outings for the economic importance in Bath of the slave trade, which made fortunes for residents and visitors alike. A little later, Bramble produces the following less than flattering list of visitors to the city:

> Every upstart of fortune, harnessed in the trappings of the mode, presents himself at Bath, as in the very focus of observation—clerks and factors from the East Indies, loaded with the spoil of plundered provinces; planters, negro-drivers, and hucksters, from our American plantations [this is pre-1776] enriched they know not how; agents, commissaries, and contractors, who have fattened, in two successive wars, on the blood of the nation; usurers, brokers, and jobbers of every kind; men of low birth, and no breeding, have found themselves suddenly translated into a state of affluence, unknown to former ages; and no wonder that their brains should be intoxicated with pride, vanity and presumption.

In 1759 an advertisement appeared in the *Bath Journal* for a thirteen-year-old black house servant—for sale. As we saw in Chapter 6, Gainsborough's work in Bath throws light on Britain's involvement in slavery and the slave trade, while a picture like "The Byam Family" suggests a close link with the wealthy society of the city. Even more explicit is William Jones' painting "The Black Boy" in the Victoria Art Gallery. The online catalogue suggests that "When this was painted, there would have been many slaves working as servants in Bath", but actual figures are hard to come by. The sitter is shown holding a basket of exotic fruit; he is said to have worked in the Pump Room but again there is no clear evidence on this point. Interestingly, the picture was given to the gallery by R. B. Dunworthy in memory of Viscountess Simon, the author of a 1930 book against slavery. This particular book was much criticized by the first wave of the civil rights movement in the US, who claimed it said much about Britain's involvement in the campaign to abolish the slave trade, but little about its role in building up the slave economy. Then, of course, there was William Beckford too—the richest man in England at one point, and another fortune based on slavery. Despite the frequent visits to Bath of leading abolitionists such as Hannah More and William Wilberforce, the city's MPs refused to present to parliament an anti-slave petition signed by over 1,000 Bath inhabitants.

Links between Bath and India are reflected in the art of the period, for example in the Victoria's "Sir Thomas Rumbold and his

Son" (c.1770) by Gainsborough. On the one hand was the polite society life of Bath, and on the other hand the less genteel enterprise of the British Empire. Rumbold was in the military service of the East India Company. He made a fortune and returned to England in 1770. He became an MP and was involved in not one, but two scandalous elections at which he was accused of bribery and corruption. And this in the pre-Reform Act period when seats were regularly bought and sold, so one assumes the amounts of money were very large and the scandal very public indeed. Reassuringly (or not), the scandals had no effect on his career as an MP or his later service in India where he was Governor of Madras from 1777 to 1780.

Bath is also implicated in the Indian Mutiny of 1857, during which widespread atrocities were committed by both Indians and the British. A tablet in St. Matthew's Church Widcombe commemorates various members of the family of General James Kennedy of the Bengal Cavalry who died after the siege of Cawnpore (now Kanpur), one of the bloodiest of all the actions of the Mutiny. Mrs. Blair and her two daughters, Susan and Isabella, lived at 13 Macaulay Buildings and worshipped at St. Matthew's. It seems that Mrs. Blair's husband had disappeared without trace during an earlier military campaign in Afghanistan, and that Mrs. Blair had gone to India in search of news about her husband.

From the middle of the twentieth century, Bath participated in the reverse demographic movement of the British Empire, the arrival of small numbers of Commonwealth immigrants in what many of them had been taught to regard as the "mother country". The West Indian migrants made a particular impact on Bath. They came to work but they also brought their cricket and their steel bands. Many of them came from Barbados. They played the pans on the boat, and on arrival for the mayor of Bath. Their first base was the YMCA in Broad Street, and despite the casual racism of 1950s England ("no blacks here"; "no coloureds need apply") they settled and thrived.

Many of the women were employed as cleaners and nurses at local hospitals, and the men in manufacturing. Afro-Caribbean people worked at the engineering firm Stothert & Pitt, one of the largest employers in the city. This is clear from their in-house magazine during this period. In 1967 a retirement photo shows two black employees, while in 1976 there is a feature about a Jamaican secretary with a university degree in French and Italian. Some of the Bath Caribbean community had come to England during the war and served in the forces: St. John Dick arrived in 1943, and had played cricket for his firm, Stothert & Pitt. In 1976 his "leisure" activity was running a Bath Multi-Racial Club with 120 members, part social club and part advice centre. But there were no black faces in that year's intake of apprentices.

Harold Ottway joined the bus company as a driver in 1956 and eventually completed forty years of service. But in neighbouring Bristol the bus company (the same company as in Bath) practised a "colour bar". In 1963 matters came to a head, led by a group of Bristolians inspired by the US civil rights movement, and in particular the bus boycott in Birmingham Alabama. Mr. Ottway recalled that on one occasion while driving on the Bath-Bristol route at the height of the dispute, a temporary bus-stop was provided on the roundabout outside Bristol Bus Station and he was asked not to drive into the bus station for fear of escalating the row. Eventually black and Asian workers were accepted in Bristol; the world did not come to an end.

The history of steel bands in Bath goes back to the formation of the Barbados All Stars in 1957 at the YMCA. Subsequently the name changed to Rainbow Steel Band and in 2007 the Rainbow Steel Orchestra celebrated its half-century with a big exhibition in the display area at the Bath Central Library. It was belated recognition of the cultural contribution that Caribbean people had made to their adopted city. One of its founders, Hallam Ifill, still plays for them. Children then followed their parents into the band, as founder members of the "travelling generation" retired from playing or moved back to Barbados. It has given concerts all over Europe as well as back home in Barbados, and also does a great deal of educational work teaching young people to play the pans.

The focus of black cricket in Bath was the popular and successful Bath West Indians cricket team. There is little doubt that they paved the way for the later popularity of Somerset's West Indian stars, Sir Vivian (Viv) Richards and Joel (Big Bird) Garner. Indeed, Richards had qualified for Somerset by playing for the famous Lansdown club in Bath in 1973. Garner was honoured in 2009 with a set of gates at the County Ground in staid Taunton. I never saw either of them play, but I did see Garry Sobers scoring a big century for the West Indies against Somerset in Bath in 1963. A big, noisy contingent of Bath West Indians was there, as was the steel band. Leastways, that is how I remember it and it is the one fact in this book that I have made no effort to check!

Orman Clarke was one of the original party of cricket- and pan-playing Barbadians who arrived in Bath in 1955. He worked at the Gas Board and later for many years in the estates department at the university. Before the university was built, he had played cricket on the playing-fields there with the Bath West Indians team, of which he was the manager. He remembered matches against one village team in particular: "We used to let Peasedown St. John win because they treated us really good when we played at their ground—the food and drink and hospitality were really super." As with the steel band, sons followed fathers into the team.

Mr. Clarke was also one of the instigators in the early 1980s of what eventually became the Bath Racial Equality Council, and later still the Community Relations Council. There had been trouble between young black men and the police and this body provided a forum for open exchange of views. "I believe I was guided to come to Bath. The Holy Spirit was saying to me, 'Go to Bath and do some work,' meaning community work," Orman Clarke wrote in a newspaper article in 2003. He died in October 2010 and the Rainbow Steel Orchestra played at his funeral service in St. John's Church at South Parade. The service was conducted by the university's Roman Catholic chaplain. I had arranged to meet him as I was completing this book, but it was not to be.

Now the West Indian elders meet at a twice-weekly lunch club called the Bath Ethnic Minorities Senior Citizens Association (BEMSCA). The three main groups there are West Indians, mainly from Jamaica and Barbados, South Asians and Chinese. Their meeting-place is Fairfield House in Kelston Road, Weston, where the Emperor of Ethiopia Haile Selassie lived from 1936 until 1941 after being deposed by Italian fascists. Bath must have been a culture shock after the land-locked time-capsule of an African kingdom over which he had exercised absolute power. But by and large he liked Bath. He watched newsreel images of Italian soldiers marching through the street of Addis Ababa at the Little Theatre. He returned on a state visit in 1954 to thank the people of Bath for their hospitality and in 1958 donated Fairfield House to the city. Now the portrait of the Lion of Judah presides over the assorted elders as they eat lunch, play dominoes and, above all, put the past to rights. It is curious, though, that this "symbol of long-neglected African identity", as Stuart Hall once called him, is celebrated in conservative, suburban Bath.

While older Caribbean people have returned home to the islands, or settled into contented old age in Bath, their children and grandchildren have continued to find it difficult to feel really at home in the city of their birth. The children find it difficult to achieve in education, while parents are anxious and mistrustful, remembering their own negative experiences of school. This sense of being "guests in their country of birth" creates an ironic contrast with middle-class white incomers to the city, who settle rapidly into jobs, membership of community organizations and activity in political and heritage groups.

New Migrants and Locals

Nowadays, migrant communities in Bath go beyond the old imperial connections. Bath has a Racial Equality Council which regularly reports on relations between the various ethnic and cultural groups in the city. Unlike larger cities—Bradford, Bolton, even Bristol—there is no one large migrant group. At the 2001 census, all black groups, both born abroad and in Bath, constituted less than one per cent of the population of the local authority area (Bath and North-East Somerset). There are similar figures for the total of people whose families come from the old imperial connections in South Asia. In all, 94 per cent are listed as white British, and the largest other group is the "other white" category—mainly from the European

Community, including the newer members such as Poland, Bulgaria and Romania. Chinese, Malaysian and Filipino communities are also present.

Some updating of the 2001 census figures in 2007 does suggest that the trend towards increased diversity in Bath has continued, though these figures do not distinguish between Bath itself and the unitary authority area of BANES. They also do not distinguish between full-time residents and the transitory and increasing student population. But given those caveats, the total BANES population has gone up by 10,000, and almost all this increase has been in groups other than "white British". The most noticeable increases are for Black African, South and East Asian groups, together with "other white" which includes North Americans, older European Union members and the new accession countries.

A major report by the Bath and North-East Somerset's Racial Equality Council in 2006 found that ethnic minority communities in the city, as in other parts of the UK, were generally to be found in low skill/low pay jobs. Many had encountered discrimination and suffered from white racism, although they might not describe it as such. This is an important point: discrimination is experienced as a private, individual or family matter, rather than a public issue. There has been no equivalent in Bath of the 1963 Bristol bus boycott mentioned above, or the 1980 riot in the St. Paul's district. Nor has there been, for that matter, any equivalent of the St. Paul's Carnival which has been running since 1967 and attracts large crowds to its noisy, colourful spectacle every year. The 2006 report also commented on the negative attitudes of the media, which prefer to comment on how migrant communities stretch public services rather than the economic contribution they make. Few people from ethnic minorities in Bath are in public leadership roles, and in general the diversity of modern Bath is tolerated rather than accepted and celebrated as a public achievement. Some may not even live in the city: the report found that while Indian people arriving in the 1980s and 1990s had professional jobs in health or engineering, there was also a hidden workforce of hotel staff who were bussed to and from London, which big hotels found cheaper than accommodating workers in the city.

Chinese people constitute a settled community in Bath, originally working in the restaurant trade. Their cultural, language and social needs are dealt with through the Bath East Asian Chinese and Friends Group, while older Chinese are active in the BEMSCA senior citizens' lunch club. They enjoy a game of mah-jong, exercise classes and listening to speakers but are less enthusiastic about the lunches... Further, Chinese culture (and that of other East Asian countries) is celebrated positively in the Museum of East Asian Art, located opposite the Assembly Rooms. There are considerable numbers of Chinese students at Bath's two universities, where they are seen as a welcome source of additional income. A second East Asian community in Bath are Filipinos, who do mainly health jobs and domestic work. The 2006 report noted that "Bath is particularly well liked by some Filipinos as it is seen as vibrant, and more accepting of international cultures compared with other parts of the UK, and with job opportunities."

Like the Filipinos, Bath's Polish community tends to be active in the Catholic Church. For both groups it constitutes a "home, away from home" and is an important source of information and social networking. Usually well educated but sometimes lacking fluency in English, they tend to do physical work, especially in the building, hotel and domestic trades, and as drivers. About one hundred work as drivers on the buses, and for many other Bathonians this is their main contact with this group of migrant workers. Their future, too, is uncertain. Many would like to go back to Poland, for example to buy houses or set up small businesses.

Bath has a mobile population, both white and non-white. It is a diverse population, but that is not to say that each of its diverse communities carries equal weight within the city. As in most places, there is a "norm" from which the "other" diverges. Today the norm is the white middle-class resident, whether born in Bath or moving into the city from outside, whether at work in a professional job or retired. They will feel involved in the day-to-day affairs of the city, will be keen supporters of its World Heritage status and of the cultural events and organizations that sustain that status. The most noticeable "other" today is not just the black or Asian migrant but more or less anyone who does not fit into the above stereotype of a normal Bathonian. They will probably live south of the river, or on the peripheral estates in Weston or Fairfield Park, or the decaying housing along the London Road. They may be homeless—an issue we shall look at briefly in Chapter 11.

Yet these other Bathonians are very far from having no cultural identity. They have their own organizations, their own social venues. They may well support Bath City Football Club or one of the many local football or rugby teams in the city rather than the prestigious Bath Rugby Club. They include the sorts of people more likely to turn up at the Rondo Theatre in Larkhall, the Mission Theatre, the Chapel Arts Centre. They may be members of the very many religious groups who are not affiliated to the official Church of England or the established non-conformists sects. They are just as likely to be seen in bars and cafés as traditional pubs. They are less likely to be seen at events organized by the Bath International Music Festival or Jane Austen Festival, more likely to attend Bath Fringe Festival events or the Widcombe Rising. Not all Bathonians think or look alike, and Bath is a much more interestingly diverse place than it may appear to the casual visitor.

Jane Austen, acerbic observer of Bath life

10 | **Bath People**
Historical Characters and Personalities

T his book has a cast of hundreds, including the many historical characters who have passed through Bath or had some
contact with the city down through the centuries. In this
chapter I have offered longer pen portraits of a few of those who
have left a lasting impression on Bath and helped to shape the beautiful city that residents and visitors alike continue to enjoy. We begin
with the mythical king and founder of the city, Bladud. Then comes
Adelard, local boy and international scholar. There are two bishops,
Oliver King and Thomas Ken, both remembered in the diocese of
Bath and Wells, albeit for rather different reasons. Next come a
cluster of those who stamped their mark on Georgian Bath: John
Wood (father and son architects), Beau Nash (Master of
Ceremonies), Ralph Allen (entrepreneur), William Oliver (a doctor
more famous for his biscuits) and finally William and Caroline
Herschel (both musicians turned astronomers). So few women? The
Wife of Bath, Selina Countess of Huntingdon, Jane Austen—all
might have been mentioned here, but are adequately covered elsewhere in the book.

Bladud: Myth of Origin
It would be idle to speculate on the dates of King Bladud, since he
exists only as a shadowy mythical figure of pre-Roman Bath. The
convoluted story of the leper king and his pigs, cured by immersion
in the healing waters of the hot springs, is central to the theory of
origin which Bath took upon itself, and so whatever the truth of the
matter, Bladud is important in Bath. But to ask whether it is true or
not is rather like asking whether the Roman tale of Romulus and
Remus is true. For those who saw an analogy between Rome, set on
its seven hills, and Bath, set among its green hills, having a royal

myth of origin mattered very much indeed.

The story in essence is very simple. Bladud was a British (Celtic) prince who contracted leprosy and was expelled from the royal court. While minding pigs somewhere in the vicinity of Bath, he noticed the fondness of the pigs for wallowing in the mud where the hot springs emerged into the Avon valley, and the way it kept them free from skin diseases. Bladud followed the pigs into the waters, was cured and returned to court. When he became king in his turn he founded the city of Bath at the place where he had been miraculously cured.

Is there historical evidence for this? In a word, no. Even suggested dates vary wildly, from the ninth century BCE to 500 BCE. Geoffrey of Monmouth introduced Bladud into his monumental *History of Britain*, which is also the source for the Arthurian legends and the character of Merlin. It is also the source for some of Shakespeare's greatest plays, notably *King Lear* and *Cymbeline*. In Monmouth's chronology, Lear was the son of Bladud. Now Bladud was up and running, just one king in a line that could be traced back to ancient Greece. If the first part of the story (the pigs) seems plausible, the second is less so. Bladud is supposed to have experimented with black magic and attempted to fly with wings attached to his arms. Not surprisingly, he died in the attempt. There was a statue of him on the pre-Georgian Guildhall in Bath, together with the equally mythical King Cole. Both statues later came to reside in Bath Street, next to the entrance to the new Bath Spa complex.

John Wood, as we have seen, was fascinated by the Bladud story. For him, classical architecture was not just the architecture of Rome, but an all-inclusive theory that integrated the temple at Jerusalem, the stone circles of the ancient Britons, the Greeks and Romans and what he himself was setting out to create in Bath. The acorns on the Circus in Bath refer both to pagan fertility myths about the oak tree, and more specifically to Bladud. When the Bath Pageant of 1909 was planned, Bladud was again to the fore, and a scene was enacted with real water and live pigs and a swineherd-king. In more recent times he inspired the highly successful public art project known as King Bladud's Pigs in Bath, and the pig mascot called Bladud at

Bath City FC. His figure still presides, as he has done for centuries, over the King's Bath, immediately below the Pump Room and the fountain at which visitors can sample the Bath water. It is quite an afterlife for a man who probably never existed.

Adelard: International Scholar

The early medieval scholar Adelard c.1080-c.1152) is a good example of a man whose life was far from circumscribed by the circle of green hills among which Bath nestled. The precise benefits of the Norman Conquest of England in 1066 are still debated. Was feudalism a good thing or not? Would it have happened any rate, with or without the arrival of the Normans? Did the benefits of closer ties with the European mainland accrue more to the ruling class rather than to the peasant? Michael Davis on the Bath Royal Scientific and Literary Institution website has no doubts about the matter: "Ten thousand Norman carpetbaggers lorded it over two million English people, having confiscated all the wealth, property and power, treating the locals with contempt." The Normans set about building a vast new cathedral in Bath, under the watchful eye of Bishop John of Tours.

Adelard was very much the "local boy who made good". We do not have detailed biographical information about him, but he probably studied at the school attached to the Benedictine monastery (later abbey) in Bath. He benefited from the extensive connections of the new Norman rulers of England with continental Europe and beyond. Specifically he benefited from the patronage of Bishop John, and in 1100 moved to the school at Tours in France, one of the great centres of learning in Western Europe. He was a polymath, and sufficiently bright to understand the limitations of Western European knowledge at the time. In particular, he was attracted by Muslim scholarship. Adelard travelled widely in the Mediterranean and Middle East and became immersed in this new learning. Western scholars knew Greek learning only in Roman translations or summaries, while Muslim scholars had access to the Greek originals. Through the reach of the Arab empire, they also absorbed learning from further afield in Persia and India.

On his return to Bath, much of Adelard's most important work involved translating texts from Arabic, which was the route by which much of the learning of ancient Greece was reintroduced to Europe in the early medieval period. He translated Euclid's *Elements of Geometry* into Latin, the common language of Western Europe and the Christian Church. It is also probable that he introduced Europe to the concept of zero, which had not been present in either Greek or Roman times. It was an important step forward in making practical calculations, for example in building, and one that we owe to Arab civilization, and beyond that the work of Hindu scholars in India.

Adelard travelled widely, in Europe and beyond, but maintained his links with Bath. He was involved in scientific work which we would now regard as rather dubious, such as astrology and alchemy, although it is now recognized that these were important sources for later work in astronomy and chemistry. He was close to the seat of power as well, as a member of Henry I's court, and therefore a government official. He was tutor to the young Prince Henry, later Henry II, to whom he dedicated a major work on astronomy.

A Tale of Two Bishops: Oliver King and Thomas Ken

King and Ken are two of the more interesting bishops who have presided over the see of Bath and Wells. While King was perhaps rather more the flamboyant, entrepreneurial figure and Ken the more reflective, spiritual figure, the man who spoke truth to power, both their careers as bishops intersect significantly with the political history of their times.

Oliver King (c.1432-1503) was chief secretary to Edward IV, but imprisoned in the Tower of London when his younger brother came to the throne as Richard III. With the accession of Henry VII in 1485, King was back in favour and became Bishop of Bath and Wells in 1495. The West Country was politically very sensitive, as it was to remain for the next two hundred years. The Cornish Rebellion of 1497, largely against unpopular taxes, garnered support throughout the area, and the rebels stopped at both Taunton and Wells on their way up to London. King's job was to secure the loyalty of Somerset to the new Tudor dynasty.

In 1499 Bishop King turned his attentions to Bath, where the Norman cathedral was in a poor state. He saw in a dream, so we are told (and this story vies with Bladud in its mythological elements), a vision of angels climbing up and down ladders stretching between earth and heaven. As the story has come down to us, he heard a voice saying "Let an Olive establish the Crown and let a King restore the Church." The story in turn inspired the famous and familiar Jacob's ladder on the west front of Bath Abbey, which has survived both restoration and wartime bombing. Working closely with the prior, William Bird, King planned a new abbey much smaller than the Norman building and occupying scarcely more space than the Norman nave, but re-using the foundations of the earlier building, as a detailed examination of the fabric will reveal. The result, with its great walls of glass and fan vaulting, marks the culmination of the perpendicular gothic style in England, on a par with King's College chapel in Cambridge or St. George's Chapel at Windsor Castle.

The vicissitudes through which Bath Abbey passed in the years of the dissolution of the monasteries and the reform of the English Church were described in Chapter 2, but what of Bishop King and Prior Bird? King died in 1503, and as a faithful servant of the king was interred in the Aldworth Chapel in St. George's at Windsor Castle. Bird lived on to 1523 and fared rather better. He was given a beautiful little chantry in the abbey, between the sanctuary and south aisle with its own miniature fan vault reflecting the ceiling high above. Bath Abbey is King's church, but it was Bird's life work, and it is fitting that he rather than King was laid to rest in the new abbey church.

Bishop Thomas Ken (1637-1711), whose prayer book for those visiting Bath to take the waters we have already noted, was a complex man who in the course of his lifetime was both rewarded and punished for his firm adherence to principle. Everything about him was different to the usual image of the politician-priest. He was brought up by his half-sister Anne and her husband the well-known fisherman Izaak Walton. Intriguingly, Walton was the biographer of another seventeenth-century divine, George Herbert, and there is something of Herbert's humility in Ken, despite the high-flying details of his early career. There is perhaps too some notion of what Herbert might have become if his poor health had not restricted him to a humble living at Bemerton, near Salisbury, and an early death.

Ken took holy orders, and served for a year at The Hague as chaplain to Princess Mary, niece of King Charles II of England and wife of the Dutch King William of Orange. William was far from the model husband, and Ken publicly rebuked him for his treatment of his wife, which may be why he was chaplain there for only a year. It may also have a bearing on his subsequent career.

Upon his return to England, he was made Royal Chaplain to King Charles II. The king had a mistress, Nell Gwyn, and for his convenience wished to lodge her in his chaplain's residence. Thomas sent a sharp refusal, on the grounds that it was not suitable that the Royal Chaplain should double as the Royal Pimp. They were strong words for anyone to address to his king, but Charles admired his honesty and bluntness, and when the bishopric of Bath and Wells became available soon after, he declared, "None shall have it but that little man who refused lodging to poor Nellie!" Ken was accordingly made a bishop. When Charles was on his deathbed, it was Ken whom he asked to be with him and prepare him for death.

So far, so good. But as we saw in the case of Bishop King, the West Country was a troublesome land. The weaving industry was not just a source of greater wealth but gave men and women a certain independence from the landowners and squires. Somerset was a hotbed of non-conformity, and had supported Parliament rather than the Crown during the Civil War. Feelings boiled over again in 1685 when the Duke of Monmouth attempted to contest the succession of James II, an acknowledged Roman Catholic. The village sign at Norton St. Philip near Bath, site of a major skirmish, refers to the Pitchfork Rebellion, but the majority of the rebels were not farm labourers but rather independent craftsmen and weavers motivated by religious sentiment, or natural rebels like Daniel Defoe. Finally at Sedgemoor, in the Somerset marshes near Bridgwater, the rebels were lured into battle and lost. Many were slaughtered in cold blood, many others taken prisoner.

Which is where Bishop Ken re-enters the story. Some prisoners were taken to the ruined palace at Wells, and held pending trial. There they found a friend in Bishop Thomas Ken who, despite obvious differences of religious opinion, ministered to them and sent messages to their families. He also wrote to the king, appealing for mercy for his people. But Lord Justice Jeffreys was on his way, determined at his Bloody Assizes to make an example of the rebels. Some 330 were executed, while 849 were transported to the slave plantations of Barbados. The splendid George Inn at Norton St. Philip was just one place where these travesties of judicial procedure took place.

There was more trouble ahead for Ken. When William and Mary came to the throne in 1689—the Glorious Revolution that was to secure England for Protestantism and, eventually, parliamentary democracy—he was deprived of his see. He had sworn an oath of allegiance to James, and was not prepared to now make a similar oath to a new king while the old king lived. A non-juror, Ken went into "exile" at Longleat House, a mansion some twenty miles southeast of Bath, under the protection of the Thynne family. The new bishop, Richard Kedder, had been chaplain to William and Mary, and was disliked by many at Wells. He and his wife were killed in their bed by a chimney falling through a roof in a storm on 26 November 1701, a fate described by other non-jurors as an act of divine providence but by Ken as a "deplorable calamity". There was a move to restore Ken to the bishopric, but he was content to see his friend George Hooper appointed. Ken stayed at Longleat, tutoring and writing poetry and hymns, some of which are still sung today. Just like those of George Herbert in fact.

Ken ordered in his will that he was to be buried in the church in the diocese of Bath and Wells closest to Longleat. This is how he comes to be buried in a strange stone dog-kennel in the churchyard against the east end wall of St. John's Church in Frome. Outside the church, that is, for the diocese would not permit him to be buried inside the church. There he stays and, some would say, rebukes a church that dealt so cruelly with the conscience of a caring priest.

Richard (Beau) Nash

Orange Grove remains one of my favourite places in the city. The view is especially good here: the obelisk, the silver birches, the sweep of the Grand Parade, the first few houses of the Bathwick estate beyond and the woods on Bathampton Down and Claverton Down—the Bath skyline again—above. The obelisk that still stands at the centre of this once fashionable corner of the city celebrates the recovery to health of William Prince of Orange in 1734 after drinking the spa waters. It bears too the name of "Richard Nash Master of Ceremonies" who paid for it. What was good for royal health was good for Bath, and what was good for Bath was good for Beau Nash. Not content with one obelisk, he erected a second, larger one in Queen Square in 1738 to commemorate the visit of Frederick Prince of Wales.

Nash (1674-1761) came from a modest background in South Wales, and progressed via grammar school (in Carmarthen) to Oxford. Here he quickly abandoned academic pursuits in favour of the social whirl—wine, women and song with a little gambling on the side. It was a good training for the life he was to lead. Having been sent down for an affair with a local woman, he perfected his social skills in London. When Nash arrived in Bath in 1705, drawn by its increasing reputation as a pleasure resort and gambling venue, he worked first under the Master of Ceremonies, Captain Webster. Within the year Webster died in a duel fought over a disputed card game, and Nash got the job, his flair for publicity appealing to the ambitious City Corporation.

As outlined earlier, during the more than half a century that he was Master of Ceremonies Nash introduced various reforms in the social and cultural life of the city. He encouraged the setting up of the first assembly rooms, and drew up rules for social behaviour for the "company" as the community of visitors and short-stay residents came to be called. There were improvements in the urban infrastructure too, and a ban on duels. On the cultural front, he brought orchestras from London to play in Bath and encouraged the private chapels which became in turn centres of musical excellence. Bath was Nash and Nash was Bath, and we have seen him involved in such activities as the founding of the Orchard Street theatre, and charitable work such as the setting up of the General Hospital.

Yet there was always a darker side to Nash. Gambling was a major cause of disorder (witness the death of Captain Webster) and difficult to deal with as both men and women within polite society were addicted to it. Indeed, gambling was central to the growth of Georgian Bath, which Bryan Little goes so far as to describe as "a sort of eighteenth-century British Las Vegas". For Beau Nash, as he came to be known, it was an important source of income. Every biographer of Nash has had to deal with the contradiction between the social order that Nash imposed on polite society in Bath and his own implication in some of the very disorderly sides of Georgian life. New laws in 1739/40 and again in 1745 restricted the number of games that could be played legally. A new game, evens and odds, was developed and Nash was involved in gaming syndicates in both Bath and Tunbridge Wells. These syndicates were exposed and Nash's reputation left in tatters. Yet remarkably he retained his job in Bath until his death, when almost immediately his friends began a largely successful attempt to rehabilitate his reputation, first with a biographical sketch by William Oliver (see below) and then with the life by Oliver Goldsmith, who emphasizes Nash's kindness and generosity.

The problems experienced by Nash from about 1740 were only partly of his own making. The world was changing, and a new moral tone was abroad. Nash, as we have seen, clashed with Wesley and came out second best. The Countess of Huntingdon and the bluestockings were reminding aristocratic Bath of their responsibilities to set moral standards for the rest of society and adhere to them. That the city fathers kept faith with Nash is a tribute to his overall success in marketing Bath as the most sophisticated city in Georgian England.

A Tale of Two Woods: John Wood the Elder and John Wood the Younger

John Wood, father and son, not only determined how Bath would look at the pinnacle of its fame as a spa and resort city, but have also generated much of the later tourist and heritage industry in the city. There is little in Wood the Elder's (1704-54) early life to suggest the grandiose. Born in Bath, the son of a local builder, he received a basic education at the Bluecoat School and was apprenticed as a carpenter. He worked in both London and Yorkshire, but by 1727 he had returned to his native city, not to enjoy its rustic Cotswold charms but to transform it into what he saw as a greater, nobler place. Was there ever a master plan, or did Wood the speculative builder make it up as he went along? What he wrote fifteen years later in his *Essay towards a Description of Bath* (1742) gives no clear indication of what was in his head in the late 1720s.

Wood was a man under the influence of two wildly different models—classical Rome and ancient Britain—which he tried to reconcile to each other. His book *The Origin of Building*, published in 1741, deals at some length with the well-known stone circle at Stonehenge and the much less well-known but equally interesting stone circles at Stanton Drew, a few miles south-west of Bath, where thoughtful modern folk still leave offerings of pebbles and flowers and nuts to celebrate the movement of the seasons. Wood traced all building back to the biblical Temple of Solomon, which he thought to be the source of both the work of ancient Britain and ancient Rome. God, according to Wood, had transmitted to Solomon a system of divine proportions, and the druids had used this in their stone circles. Bladud, in this imaginative reading, was no longer a mythological figure but a key historical figure linking ancient Britain with the Mediterranean world of Jews, Greeks and Romans.

According to his 1742 book, Wood wanted to develop three areas: the land owned by Dr. Gay (remembered in the name of Gay Street) north-west of the city centre, the old abbey orchards southeast of the centre, and the Bathwick lands across the river. As we have seen, the Bathwick developments did not take place until the end of the eighteenth century. Queen Square was built on Dr. Gay's land, and North and South Parades on the old abbey lands, but in neither case did what was actually built measure up to Wood's ambitions. Each of these three areas was to have its Royal Forum (or square), its Grand Circus and its Gymnasium. Only Dr. Gay's land, with Queen Square and the Circus, even approached these ambitions. The Parades are especially suggestive of the gap between ambition and achievement. Features such as Corinthian detailing on the central blocks of each parade were omitted, but what was provided was a significant extension to Bath's visitor accommodation, and wide, flagstoned pavements which allowed well-dressed visitors to promenade without the inconvenience of being splashed by Somerset mud.

Wood's magical and murky theory of architectural history ("a fantastic farrago of imagination and nonsense", according to John Haddon) is hard to reconcile with the splendid buildings for which he was responsible: Queen Square, North and South Parades, the Circus, the General Hospital, Prior Park, the cottages for Ralph Allen's workers at Combe Down—plus two buildings that have not survived: St. Mary's Chapel at Queen Square and Gainsborough's house in the Abbey Churchyard. Yet wild theory and sober practice are not entirely divorced. The Circus and the Royal Crescent may be read as symbols of sun and moon, the same sun and moon worshipped by the ancients, and which continue to rise and fall above Bath's Georgian buildings. The dimensions of the Circus approximate to the stone circles at Stonehenge and Stanton Drew. The decorative symbols at the Circus are derived from both alchemy and freemasonry and suggest a world very different from the rationalist, scientific world that the eighteenth century was growing towards.

Of John Wood the Younger (1728-81) we know much less. As a young man he supervised the building of a town hall at Liverpool to his father's design. He completed the Circus, and was largely responsible for the Royal Crescent, even granted that his father may have had the initial notion of a linked circle and crescent. In style the Crescent suggests some distance between father and son, a full-blown neoclassical conception with giant pillars rising the full height of the upper storeys, and an absence of decorative features, whether alchemical, masonic or otherwise. Just east of the Circus, John Wood the Younger was responsible for the new (upper) Assembly Rooms, while down in the town centre he designed the Hot Bath, now neatly incorporated into the new spa buildings. Like his father, he designed one of Bath's lost private chapels—the gothic Margaret Chapel in Margaret's Buildings, just off Brock Street which links Circus and Royal Crescent. Yet the son did not have the business acumen of the father, and he died in 1781 at Batheaston surrounded by debts. Both father and son are buried at Swainswick church, on the eastern out-skirts of Bath.

Ralph Allen: Humble Entrepreneur

Ralph Allen (1693-1764) shares his humble background with John Wood the Elder and Richard Nash. Together, the trio reveal the po-tential for entrepreneurship and social climbing in eighteenth-century Bath. In his life he made and enjoyed two fortunes. He was born in St. Columb Major in Cornwall and from an early age was linked with the post office, a vanguard industry of the century. His grandmother is reputed to have kept the post office in St. Columb; by 1708 the young Allen was working in the office at Exeter and by 1710 in Bath. In 1712, at the age of just nineteen, he was deputy postmaster there. By 1720 he had won the right to control the revenue from all the cross-country posts (i.e. those not passing through London), which proved as profitable, perhaps more prof-itable, than the young Allen had anticipated. He was thorough and careful, a man with an eye for detail.

Acquiring the rights to a major government monopoly in this way required political friends, and Allen was good at making friends. He worked from home, in the splendid house that can still be seen off Lilliput Alley, just round the corner from the abbey. He married well, and it was from his brother-in-law that he acquired the land on which he was to build Prior Park and build his second fortune—from the Bath stone industry. He was a close ally of George Wade, sent to Bath to secure support for the Hanoverian king, George I, in 1714, and subsequently its member of parliament. Wade and Allen worked together on the scheme to open up river transport between Bath and Bristol, a development that was to prove decisive for ship-ping stone from the quarries. The missing link between quarries and River Avon was provided by the new tramway down what is now

Ralph Allen Drive, following the external wall of the Prior Park estate.

Allen worked closely with John Wood the Elder, who provided a new façade for Allen's town house, and, as Allen's fortune grew, was chosen as the architect of the great new mansion on the hills above the city. Whatever was going on in Bath, the names of Nash, Wood and Allen were always to the fore. They served as a guarantee to the Corporation that whatever the project it would probably be in the interest of the people of Bath as well as certainly in the interests of the Corporation—and certainly would line the pockets of the three men. Not that Allen left much to chance. He became successively freeman, council member and mayor of the city.

Then there was William Pitt. Unlikely as it may seem, Allen's Palladian Bridge in Prior Park gardens, modelled on previous examples at Stowe and Wilton, was probably a political gesture, marking out support for a group of Whig politicians known as the Boy Patriots. If so, it worked: the bridge was completed in 1755 and Pitt became MP for Bath in 1757. It was not always an easy relationship. In particular, Allen slipped up by securing a loyal address from the Corporation to the king (by now George III) congratulating him on the Peace of Paris in 1763. The terms of the treaty were vehemently opposed by Pitt, who retaliated by selling his house in the Circus and severing his connections with the city. When Allen died the following year, he left one thousand pounds in his will to Pitt as a gesture of reconciliation.

Allen's aims were not just economic but cultural too. He formed an alliance with Alexander Pope, who designed the first upper gardens at Prior Park along the lines of the better known gardens at Stourhead. These have been recently restored by the National Trust, the owners of the gardens. Pope referred to Allen in a poem of 1738 as "low-born", later changing this to the less pejorative "humble". Like other writers of the mid-century, especially Henry and Sarah Fielding, he had reason to be grateful for Allen's generous patronage, whatever the circumstances of his Cornish birth. Equally grateful were the workers at the quarry on Combe Down for whom Allen provided some of the best workers' housing of Georgian England.

Which William Oliver?

It is curious that two doctors, both named William Oliver, and both Cornishmen, are implicated in the eighteenth-century medical controversies surrounding the Bath waters. So curious, in fact, that the suggestion has even been made that the second William Oliver was the illegitimate son of the first. The first William Oliver (1658-1716), before qualifying as a doctor, was a surgeon to Monmouth's troops in the 1685 rebellion. He escaped, completed his studies and subsequently published in 1704 *A practical essay on fevers, containing remarks on the hot and cold methods of their cure,* which included "A dissertation on the hot waters of Bathe", later expanded as *A practical dissertation on Bath waters; to which is added a relation of a very extraordinary sleeper near Bath* (1707). I shall leave the reader to enquire further about the sleeper. For his labours, he received a memorial in Bath Abbey and the unkind assertion that he had fathered the second William Oliver.

The splendid portrait by William Hoare of our second William Oliver (1695-1764), with a colleague Mr. Peirce, examining three candidates for admission to the General Hospital in Bath, still hangs in that hospital, in the creation of which Oliver was a prime mover. Built to a design by John Wood the Elder, the impact of the façade was unfortunately much weakened by the addition of a heavy third storey in the 1790s. Buildings speak of their times and few more loudly than this one. Wood gave his services free, Ralph Allen gave the stone, Beau Nash and his chums raised subscriptions. Painters gave paintings on suitable medical and miraculous subjects. It made good sense as a lodging house for poorer visitors to the hot springs, putting a certain distance between wealthy visitors to the city and the poor, a constant preoccupation of Georgian Bath. Dr. Oliver was a sophisticated man, an intimate of Pope, and on easy terms with other Bath notables such as Nash, Allen and Wood, all of whom were keen supporters of the hospital. In 1740 he became the first director of the hospital, with Peirce as his surgeon.

Just across the road, in Trim Street, behind the only surviving fragment of Bath's medieval wall, there is a plaque on the wall:

> This piece of ground was in the year 1736 set apart for the burial of patients dying in the Bath General Hospital. And after receiving 238 bodies was closed by the governors of that charity in the year 1849, from regard to the health of the living.

So did immersion in the Bath waters, or the drinking of the Bath waters, cure illness? R. S. Neale in his social history of Bath is scornful. Bath attracted the rich, idle and gullible, and the "easy optimism of its doctors and apothecaries" encouraged them to think that cures for the excesses of their lives—too much food and drink, too little exercise, too little personal hygiene, too much casual sex—were at hand. There was money in medicine, and as we saw in the case of Gainsborough, painting the portrait of your doctor was one of the few ways available of avoiding the bills. Oliver wrote sparingly of the curative qualities of Bath waters, especially in cases of gout. Yet his life and work suggest that it was the good company of Bath, the general sociability of the place, that raised the general spirits of visitors, and thus constituted the cure. In short, being on holiday with like-minded people of similar class and tastes does you good.

Oliver was a shrewd businessman as well as a doctor. Go to the Pump Room, taste the waters. Can you imagine a more unpleasant flavour? In consequence, as the emphasis shifted away from bathing towards drinking the spa water, Oliver perfected a thin digestive biscuit that could be eaten with the water, and which might take the edge off its taste. The Bath Oliver was born. It is little use asking for the original recipe: any documents relating to the history of the biscuit were lost when Fortt and Son, who manufactured the biscuit into the 1960s, were bombed in the Bath blitz of 1941. None of his medical knowledge and skills prevented Oliver from falling prey to gout; he is buried in the churchyard at Weston, with memorials in both All Saints Church in the village and in the abbey.

As for the hospital that he helped to found, despite the fond local name of the "Min" (Mineral Water Hospital), its correct name is now the Royal National Hospital for Rheumatic Diseases. It has a hydrotherapy pool, but does not use spa waters. The National Health Service ceased to use the spa waters in the 1970s, and if there is any restorative property in the new spa, it is surely a continuation of the spirit of the Romans that immersion in water is a pleasant and sociable experience. As for drinking the stuff, it is no doubt as good or as bad for you as any spring water, but no spring water tastes half as awful. Cue a plate of Bath Oliver biscuits.

Happy Families: Caroline and William Herschel

It was not only Wales and Cornwall that contributed to the flowering of Georgian Bath. Caroline and William Herschel came from a large, musical family in Hanover, North Germany. Young William (1738-1822) followed his father into the band of the Hanoverian guards. Given the close connections between Hanover and England—the royal family was after all from Hanover too—he found himself stationed in England during his teens, and learned some English. But music was the universal language, and on his return to England, Herschel rapidly gained a reputation as a composer and performer. In 1766 he was appointed organist at the newly opened Octagon Chapel in Bath. The organ which Herschel played was inaugurated in 1767 with a performance of Handel's Messiah. His younger sister Caroline (1750-1848) came to Bath to keep house for him from 1772, stayed, took singing lessons, and sang in concerts with her brother in both Bath and Bristol. Later she followed him into astronomy, first as his assistant, later as an astronomer in her own right.

"She followed him". There is more to it than that, for this is a Cinderella story without a handsome prince. At home in Hanover, her mother had used her as a domestic drudge. William helped her to build a creative career for herself in Bath, but she remained at his beck and call. So as his own interests turned to astronomy he expected her to follow. One imagines her easily sitting at the wide open window in New King Street (now the Herschel Museum) on cold winter nights recording her brother's astronomical findings as he searched the heavens with some success. He discovered a new planet: Uranus. In 1782 Herschel received royal recognition and a pension and moved with Caroline to a new home near Windsor Castle. Eventually he married, and Caroline was left alone. In her memoirs (she lived long enough to write two separate versions) she complained of being put upon and unloved, short of both friends and money.

William's astronomical views were rather extraordinary. He believed, for example, in the theory of "Plenitude". On this reckoning, the universe was more than Newton's clockwork mechanism: rational beings existed throughout the universe. So far, so good, but he rather spoilt it for the modern reader by placing at least some of those rational beings on the moon and sun. In many ways Caroline seems the more scientific figure of the two, with her careful recording and accurate calculations. She was famous as the discoverer of comets and nebulae. After William's death, she viewed the future with trepidation as a "chamber of death" where she might reflect on her "isolated situation". She lived for 25 years more, received the gold medal of the Astronomical Society of London, and when her much loved nephew John Herschel, Professor of Astronomy at Cambridge, visited her, he found her cheerful and relaxed. But on paper she continued to emphasize the negative. A new version of her memoirs, written in her nineties, keeps all the pessimism in. A complex woman, then, who despite her small physical stature (she was only 4 feet 9 inches tall, probably as a result of smallpox in childhood) achieved fame in the profession her brother had chosen for her, and lived to the age of 98 years.

Bath by night

11 | **The Dark Side**
Death, Vice and Social Problems

"Snobs, rogues, poseurs, charlatans, grotesque popinjays and prepos-
terous valetudinarians have mingled always with the virtuous, and re-
lieved the lovely city of perfection."

Jan Morris, foreword to *By the Waters of Sul*, 1997

If building the perfect Jerusalem has long been the ambition of
town planners and religious idealists, then as Jan Morris suggests, perfection can also be rather dull. Fortunately Bath has
seldom been either perfect or dull. It has a long history of attracting
not only flamboyant charlatans, but also vagrants, miscreants, and
the poor in search of a better life away from their home village. Some
of these made a success of life in Bath, but not all.

Drownings in the River Avon have been frequent through its
history, and it is often difficult to know if these were the result of
drunkenness, crime or suicide. The case of Mary Brown in 1845, as
recounted by Graham Davis and Penny Bonsall in their excellent
history of Bath sub-titled "Image and Reality", may be taken as ex-
emplary. A labourer's wife, Brown was regularly drunk, and also in
the habit of taking other men back to her lodgings. On the evening
in question, she was drunk and abusive. She left the pub at 11.30
with a group of men. The following morning her body was fished
out of the river: the verdict was death by drowning, but it was never
determined how she got into the river.

Suicide was much more common in eighteenth- and nineteenth-century England, given the depths of poverty into which it
was possible to fall with little in the way of a safety net. The killing
of young babies was also alarmingly frequent, mostly as a result of
servants or young prostitutes giving birth with no real prospect of
being able to care for the child. For many in Bath outside the

charmed circle of fashionable society, life could only be described as short and brutish. In 1841 the average gentleman or professional died aged 55; for labourers and artisans it was less than half that figure—24 and 25 years being their life expectancy. Both cholera and smallpox were endemic in Bath, with outbreaks centred inevitably on the crowded slums of Avon Street and Corn Street.

Alcohol was undoubtedly a factor in many crimes, both casual and serious, but while pubs were blamed by the local press and the police as centres of evil, they were also places where working people could find out about jobs and housing. They also served as meeting places for the various clubs and societies which working-class people were beginning to establish to give themselves at least an element of social insurance. It is a duller subject than murder, suicide, drunkenness, prostitution or even epidemics, and perhaps for that reason has been less studied. At the other end of the social spectrum, gambling was a major source of disorder, and difficult to deal with as both men and women within polite society were addicted to it.

Prostitution was a major industry in the city, and accepted as such. Smollett referred to the prostitutes as the "nymphs of Avon Street". Fines for keeping a brothel were tiny in relation to those exacted in the late eighteenth century for keeping a private gambling den. Village girls attracted to Bath by the prospect of employment, and then not finding it, often ended up as prostitutes as only those resident in the city for five years were entitled to Poor Law relief. It was an irony that visitors were just as likely to acquire venereal diseases in Bath as find a cure for them.

The sex industry in Georgian Bath was complemented by the growth of pornography, centred on James Leake, the city's main printer and bookseller. Leake was brother-in-law to Samuel Richardson and the owner of Bath's largest circulating library as well as a bookshop in Terrace Walk. There was no rigid boundary between general literature and pornography, at least until the mid-century.

Dens of Iniquity

The history of social disorder in Bath overlaps with the history of its pubs, as Andrew Swift and Kirsten Elliott explain in *Awash with Ale*.

It only claims to be a history of the city's pubs; but if you only have time to read one book about the real history of Bath, read this one. The authors depend greatly on newspaper reports of both the eighteenth and nineteenth centuries. These very detailed stories suggest the extent of crime in the city, and its close relation to three activities: gambling, prostitution and drinking. In many cases, pubs were the places where quarrels would degenerate into fights, often with the use of knives, and also where casual liaisons with prostitutes would be made.

Just one example suggests how these various activities were related. In 1850 Fanny Hooper, a Bath woman, was charged with having stolen money from Henry Silver. He had approached her in Westgate Street, taken her for a drink in a pub in Westgate Buildings and thence to the King's Head, where he purchased more drink and the use of a bed. She later left with the contents of his purse. The case of Fanny Hooper was dismissed for lack of evidence, leaving her client out of pocket and the object of ridicule.

Punishments often seemed quite disproportionate to the crime. The old forms of punishment by public mockery (the stocks; the pillory) were gradually replaced by criminal laws which made prison sentences, hanging and transportation the common punishments for petty crimes—the crimes of poverty such as stealing a loaf of bread— as well as serious crimes such as murder. Swift and Elliott write that at the 1853 Quarter Sessions three people were sentenced to transportation, one for stealing a turkey, one for stealing a hammer and the third for stealing a pair of trousers. (I am pleased to say that the only strand of my own North Somerset family who left for Australia in the nineteenth century went under their own steam and paid their way.) The police found it especially difficult to maintain law and order during periods when the city was crowded: the annual fair, election time, the horse-races at Lansdown.

Methodism and the Struggle against Vice

To return to Georgian Bath, the history of vice is part and parcel of the story of the rise of Methodism in the city, and for that reason the activities of this important denomination find a larger place here

THE DARK SIDE

than in the chapter which deals with religion. John Wesley famously declared that Bath was "that Sodom of the land". More explicitly he wrote: "Is it possible? Can the Gospel have place where Satan's throne is?" (*At Satan's Throne* was the title of Bruce Crofts' book on Methodism in Bath.) Bath was the fourth Methodist society to be formed, after London, Bristol and Kingswood, and Wesley made up to one hundred visits to Bath from 1739 onwards, especially in the early years of the movement. Wesley, as we noted in Chapter 8, preached at the Countess of Huntingdon chapel in the Vineyards, but kept a much greater distance than she did between himself and the dancers and drinkers, gossips and gamblers of fashionable Bath, despite the fact that not only the poor and downtrodden but also the rich and fashionable attended his meetings. He preached to large crowds, often in the open air. On a field in the vicinity of present Manvers Street he faced down Beau Nash who queried his authority to preach in this way. "You, Mr. Nash, take care of your body, we take care of our souls, and for the food of our souls we come here." Such was Wesley's parting shot.

From a hired room in Corn Street the Methodists progressed to a site in Avon Street, in the heart of that troubled district we have been describing. In 1777 Wesley referred to "the chapel in the midst of sinners where I have never heard an immodest word—but prayers and blessings in abundance". From the opening of the Countess of Huntingdon chapel in 1765, this tended to attract the more prosperous supporters of the new piety, while the poor resorted to Avon Street. Like the bluestockings, the countess saw her specific mission as being to arouse the consciences of the upper classes, though of course the bluestockings remained attached to the established church and saw Methodism as a dangerous and potentially subversive sect. There is without doubt some cross-over between the rise of Methodism in Bath and its reputation for radical politics in the first half of the nineteenth century. Yet below a certain level in society, vice and crime continued unchecked, as the two examples mentioned earlier in this chapter suggest. Indeed, patterns of crime widened, as Bath became a more populous city with a wider social base and the beginnings of industry. It was much the same mixture of mugging, pickpocketing and burglary that Charles Dickens knew so well. And Charles Dickens knew Bath well too.

By the middle of the nineteenth century Methodism had become a divided movement. In Bath, the Wesleyan and Primitive Methodists had roughly equal numbers of adherents, with smaller numbers attending the Free Methodist chapel in Lower Borough Walls. To what extent these divisions may have reduced Methodism's effectiveness in speaking out over social issues is a matter of conjecture. Later in the century there was also competition from the Salvation Army with its street bands and marching which appealed to young people in the city. Bruce Crofts refers to "staid Christians including many Methodists" who were suspicious of, or even hostile towards, this new organization. Some Methodist activities were doubtless inward-looking, for example the eight Bands of Hope containing 767 members who had "signed the pledge" of temperance. To set against that, in 1897 money was collected for famine relief in India and to support the families of striking Welsh miners.

By now, the Church of England had discovered the urban poor. It built new churches, but also welcomed within its ranks clergymen determined to take religion at face value and attempt to live out their beliefs in their action. It was an Anglican priest, Jay Bolton of St. James', who became involved in one of the great set-pieces of action against immorality in Victorian Bath. The Wesleyans sent messages of support to this "cause of justice, morality and purity" but it was Bolton and his supporters at St. James' who were making all the noise. After two years of agitation, Bolton eventually wrote a pamphlet, published in 1884, about this affair, and the account here follows closely his own.

The centre of the dispute was a squalid slum area called St. James' Court where some sixty prostitutes were operating from twenty houses in the vicinity of the Bell Inn. In vain the vicar tried to get the City Council and the police to take action. Bolton emphasized that this public nuisance had been going on for years, attracting young women and their clients from other parts of the town and the surrounding villages. Seeing it as a social, economic and religious issue for local people, he refers to the "old dissipation of this city years ago", perhaps an allusion to the period of Wesley and Nash. "By day, even on Sundays, and within a stone's throw of St James's Church, dissolute women, half-dressed, would stand in groups soliciting passers-by. At night, riots, fighting, and piano-playing disturbed the whole area. Respectable people were ashamed to live in or pass through such a district." Was it affecting church attendances and therefore income? Probably.

Parishioners themselves brought two successful prosecutions. They tried and failed to have the Bell closed, but eventually the authorities revoked its licence. The overall purpose of the church activity was not just to rid the area of a nuisance, but to "save" the women (it is not stated what the aim was in relation to their male clients). Here the long-established "Female Home and Penitentiary" at Ladymead House in modern Walcot Street played a major role, just a few yards along from a charity shop now run to support Bath Women's Refuge. Set up in 1805, the penitentiary had a chapel added in 1845, replacing an earlier isolation ward for women suffering from syphilis. Bolton's booklet claimed 34 rescues of which 27 were described as "satisfactory". Many of the women ended up in service. One woman is described as "an owner and keeper of four houses of ill fame in St James's Court. After much persuasion she sold them to St James's Trustees, and is now living a consistent life with her husband (…) Since her reformation, this person has had four of her children baptised." Looking to the future, Bolton envisaged the purchase and demolition of the whole court, and using the law to oppose prostitution in other parts of the city.

By the end of the nineteenth century, the broad distinction in working-class Bath was between those hard-working families who regarded themselves as "respectable" and those families classified as "rough". But there was no single way of drawing the line between rough and respectable. Thus a man who held down a job during the week but got drunk consistently on a Saturday night might be judged to belong to either group, depending on the day of the week. Davis and Bonsall make considerable use of material from a woman called Louie Stride who lived long enough to record her experiences. Born in 1907, the illegitimate daughter of a prostitute, she recalls her mother being hounded out of a cottage at the back of a sweet-shop in Holloway by her neighbours. Davis and Bonsall comment: "Yet Holloway, viewed from without and from the perspective of the dominant middle-class culture, was seen as a homogenous district in terms of socio-economic structure and cultural values… it was perceived as 'poor' and 'rough'." Later Louie's mother married a Canadian soldier, which entitled her to a regular income while he was away on active service in the First World War.

The Impact of War

So far in this chapter we have referred to problems arising, as it were, on the home front. The First and Second World Wars proved that devastation could also come from outside. For many men, it was the First World War that first took them outside the confines of the city. Many, of course, never returned; others survived but moved away. The raw statistics give some idea of the impact of the war on Bath. In total, 11,213 enlisted in the armed services out of a population of 70,000; over 1,000 were killed. Hospitals were rapidly expanded to take the wounded; the Bath War Hospital was opened at Combe Park in 1915 with ten fifty-bed huts adjoining the Lansdown cricket ground. By 1918 its capacity was 1,800. Local factories such as Stothert & Pitt were turned over to war work, with munitions providing employment to over 2,000 men and 1,000 women. It was under these circumstances that women obtained access to a broader labour market, and although there was some return to home and domestic work after the war, it was the beginning of a process which by the end of the twentieth century was to provide a high degree of equality of opportunity for women, if not equality of pay.

Bath is fortunate in having a fine history of the First World War, Andrew Swift's *All Roads Lead to France*. It emphasizes that while the war affected the country as a whole, its impact reached down into every city, every town, every village in the land. Bath would never be the same again. The suffering of those who fought was matched by the shortages, the constant worry about family members on active service, the new and unfamiliar roles that people were called on to play. While more aristocratic versions of the war often contrast the appalling conditions in which men fought and died on the Western Front with life continuing much as usual back home, this was not how it was experienced by most ordinary families.

One Bath soldier who became famous in the present century as the final survivor of the trenches on the Western Front was Harry Patch, who died in 2009. For nearly eighty years he kept his own counsel. Finally, after his hundredth birthday, he spoke about the horrors of war, describing it as "organized murder and nothing else". Born at Combe Down, he is buried in the churchyard at Monkton Combe, just a few yards from Church Cottages where my mother spent her childhood.

Harry Patch's memoirs extend to the Second World War when he was a fire-watcher in the city during the so-called Baedeker raids. He had caustic remarks to make on various aspects of that war, including the extent of black market activities. Certainly, experiences of wartime in Bath varied from family to family. Those with gardens and allotments, or those who kept hens or had relations in the country villages around, were more likely to have continuing access to fresh food, though in fact the main shortages occurred after rather than during the war. Worst of all were the bombings—300 killed and 19,000 homes damaged. For those who had family members serving abroad, or were bombed out of their houses, or had relations killed in the bombing, these were harrowing times indeed. One of the most moving stories of the war comes from a German—Willi Schludecker, the last surviving member of the German Luftwaffe squadron to bomb Bath, who died in 2010. In 2008 he visited Bath for a memorial service at the Shaftesbury Road Memorial Gardens in Oldfield Park, and echoed Harry Patch's words when he declared that "War is madness".

Homelessness

During the war many people were made homeless as a result of bomb damage. In the 1980s homelessness again became a feature of Bath life, but did not elicit the same sort of massive public response as in wartime and post-war Bath: rebuilding, renovating and creating new homes for people. Alcoholism and drug addiction exacerbate the problem of homelessness, but there are major issues related to Bath's success as a city: the fact that is a desirable place to live, rising house values and therefore rents, the selling off of council housing stock and the very low priority given to investment in new social housing in the city. And of course there are all those students, many of them living in traditional areas of working-class housing such as Oldfield Park. This provides the essential background to the *Big Issue* sellers and beggars who are a feature of everyday life.

Julian House, with its very professional Board of Management and paid staff, is a charity which was set up in 1987 after the much publicised death of a rough sleeper. Their night shelter in Manvers Street offers basic dormitory beds for up to 21 people. There are still rough sleepers, of course, who will not use the shelter, and others who prefer "lily-padding", which sounds lovely but involves moving around from one friend's sofa or floor to another. These are humiliating and unsatisfactory ways of life for perfectly ordinary people who have fallen on hard times. Funding was obtained a few years back for a proper hostel for the homeless in the city but for complicated reasons a satisfactory location was never found and the dormitory at Manvers Street remains the only option for over two hundred and fifty people every year. In addition, a major part of the work of Julian House is working with individuals and families who are in danger of being made homeless because of losing their jobs, getting into rent arrears, the break-up of long-term relationships and family groups.

Apart from Julian House, local churches maintain a concern for the homeless. This includes financial donations to Julian House, providing cheap daytime meals on their premises and the nightly soup and clothes run at the back of the Podium car-park (ironically next door to the Hilton hotel). This facility is funded and staffed in turn by the various city churches. The outlook is bleak. In late 2010 both Peter Price, Bishop of Bath and Wells, and Ken Loach, film-director, made their own separate analyses of the prospects for the homeless. Re-launching the Julian House bookshop in Walcot Street, Loach pointed to the increased demands likely to be made on Julian House and similar organizations by cuts in spending on welfare: "We

THE DARK SIDE

can't be a 'pass the hat round' society," he said. "We are a very wealthy country and the idea that it is the poor that have to pay is not acceptable." Meanwhile in the rather more up-market setting of the House of Lords, Bishop Peter was explaining that government spending cuts could leave hundreds of thousands of people homeless in the coming years. He emphasized how the craze for second homes in beautiful rural Somerset complicates any attempt to build community: "Families who may be key players in local communities will lose their long-term security, and individuals will lose their social networks and relationships of mutual support and care if they have to move. Where will they move to? It is these very communities and networks that provide the relationships for a civic society, whether 'big' or not."

Homelessness is just one of the challenges facing Bath in the future. As we saw in Chapter 4, it has had particular problems in recent years in dealing with large-scale projects which raise tensions between its role as a local service centre and as a major destination of international tourism. It remains to be seen if the latest council structure (Bath and North-East Somerset unitary authority) will be any more successful than its predecessors in dealing with major issues affecting the city. The loss of the Dyson Engineering Design School was a severe blow to those who want to keep the remnants of productive industry alive in the city. Bath's loss has been London's gain, with £5 million donated by the Dyson Foundation towards the cost of new Royal College of Art buildings in Battersea. In addition there are the more mundane problems that affect many big cities. Open the local papers any week and you will read stories of vandalism, street drinking and drunken scenes in city streets, all night student parties, theft, muggings and worse. The local press has thrived for over a century on "bad news" stories about the city, but each of these stories, however blown out of proportion and context, is a real problem for the victim or victims, or those who just prefer a quiet life.

Hope for the Future

It is not an easy moment to be optimistic about the future. And that old chestnut "Who is Bath for?" has again been given public exposure. At a public meeting of the Better Bath forum in October 2010, the following questions were suggested for discussion: "Is the visitor economy growing at the expense of residents? Do new developments threaten local communities? Are the less well-off benefiting as much as other people? Is the city becoming over commercialised? Are we doing enough for young people? What needs to be done differently?" Good questions, but even supposing generally agreed answers were forthcoming, what prospect is there in the short-to-middle-term future of relevant actions being taken? Meanwhile consultation was also proceeding on priorities for the World Heritage Site, but again with no clear idea of whether money would be available to back plans agreed.

To find a project where somehow rulers and ruled seem reconciled to one another, it is necessary to leave the city centre for the airy heights of Combe Down. Combe Down has only been part of the city since 1961, but its place in Bath's history has been secure since Ralph Allen developed the stone mines here in the eighteenth century. Ralph Allen's quarries have returned to haunt Combe Down, not to mention Bath and North-East Somerset Council, who feared they might be left to pick up the bill. The problems arose in the twentieth century as more and more homes, both private and council houses, were built on Combe Down above the now abandoned caverns left by the quarrymen. At first, the plan was simply to fill the tunnels and caverns with PFA (pulverised fuel ash from power stations) but local residents objected to possible health risks, and eventually, some six years later, it was agreed to fill the caverns with foam concrete, with central government footing most of the enormous bill. But this is Bath, and heritage intervened again and rather unexpectedly in the form of colonies of rare greater horseshoe bats found to be living in the worked out quarries. So alongside the filling, large amounts of money have been spent shoring up some caverns so that the bats will have a home for the foreseeable future. It will also, hopefully, add to the places of interest for visitors to the city.

The project, covering 62 acres of shallow mines and involving 250 workers, many of them ex-miners from South Wales, required the pouring of approximately 750,000 cubic yards of concrete, and has been one of the biggest such projects in the world. Ten miles of underground roadways were built during the process. It has drawn not just on modern technology, but on the local knowledge of older residents of Combe Down. Guided tours have featured, and the arts have risen to the challenge in the form of music, photography, film, pottery and a Combe Down pageant, to soften the hard edges of such a major undertaking and a major disruption of people's daily lives. Andy Croft, a poet working with local schools and people, paid tribute to the poems written by local people and included in the project anthology *Time in the Shape of a Mine*: "These poets are like miners, digging down through seams of memory laid down a long time ago and bringing back great beautiful lumps of understanding and imagination." Now the Firs Field, Combe Down's main recreational area and the headquarters of the filling operation, has been re-sown with grass seed; now the residents of Combe Down, clutching their commemorative plates, can return to their own abnormal normality but with a deepened sense of their own history, which is only in part the history of Bath.

I am only sorry that my mother, a simple woman who loved poetry, brought up just down the road in Monkton Combe, and who attended Combe Down School, did not live long enough to make her own contribution to the project. There is in Bath a sense of the permanence of the earth, of the fleeting folly of human ambition, of great and small humbled by the relentless tugging of history. There is that in Andy Croft's words too:

Time, time in the shape of an hour
Round which the seconds slowly pass,
Time, time in the shape of an hour
Like centuries slipping through the glass.
Time, time in the shape of an hour.

Prior Park

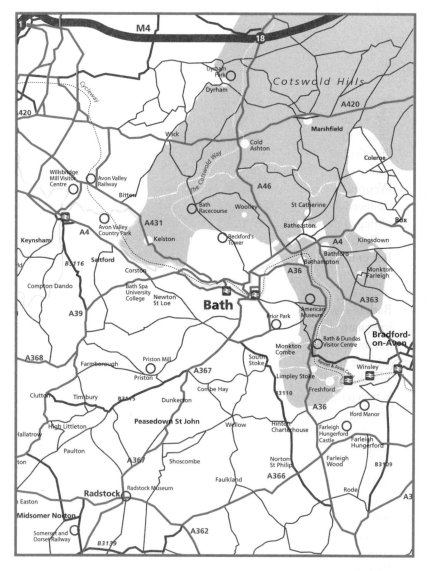

Bath and its surroundings

12 | **Escape**
Suburbs and Surroundings

ath is not just the city centre, or even the splendid Georgian and Regency housing climbing the slopes of Lansdown. In this chapter we look at the vigorous, sometimes idiosyncratic life of villages that have been absorbed into the urban fabric but have also managed to retain a separate identity: Widcombe, Batheaston, Weston, Combe Down and Twerton. Next we return to a theme introduced at the very beginning of the book: Bath in its semi-rural setting of the surrounding hills—Lansdown, Claverton Down (home to Bath University and the American Museum) and Solsbury Hill. But unlike the Wife of Bath we shall stray no further

Urban Villages

Bath is a city of villages. Hemmed in by its walls, it once shared the irregularly shaped valley floor, and its many springs and brooks, with a number of villages. While these have now all been incorporated into the city limits as suburbs, each retains a rather separate identity, and there is both pride in local identity and often strong rivalry between them. Bath overall has managed to avoid becoming simply one large urban conglomeration.

Widcombe, just across the river behind Bath Spa station, is the closest to the city centre and perhaps for that reason the keenest to hold on to its separate identity. During the nineteenth century Bath and Widcombe were linked most directly by a wooden "halfpenny" toll bridge immediately behind the station. The bridge was well used, and in June 1877 disaster struck. The Bath and West Show Society was celebrating its centenary at Beechen Cliff, and the bridge was crowded with passengers who had just got off a train from Weymouth and were heading for the show. The structure collapsed without warning, and ten people were killed and over fifty injured.

The bridge was rebuilt and still serves as an important walking route from Lyncombe and Widcombe into Bath. There is a fine little stone toll house, marked on its river face with the flood levels from the many times when the impatient Avon has burst its banks.

Widcombe is a lively place to live and boasts the largest residents' association in the city. For many years it has been home to the Natural Theatre Company, which specializes in street theatre and happenings of all kinds. The company supervises (if that is the right word) the biennial Widcombe Rising, now Bath's premier street festival. As we saw in Chapter 7, an event more different from the rather stately Bath International Music Festival is hard to imagine. In recent years Widcombe has also acquired its own Mummers. This ancient tradition has been kept alive in the area, most notably at Marshfield, just over the border in Gloucestershire. Here the Marshfield Paper Boys and Marshfield Brass Band perform every Boxing Day morning, much as they have done for about eighty years. Marshfield shared in that long depression in English agriculture that only ended with the Second World War and the sudden need for the country to become self-sufficient in food. The Marshfield Mummers' Play was an early example of community arts, encouraged by an active member of Cecil Sharp's English Folk Song and Country Dance Society—revival, re-creation and reinvention are all involved. At Widcombe the Mummers are rather freer with tradition, introducing characters such as Busometa in celebration of the new bus station just across the river, and songs such as "Widcombe You're a Jewel". The play is performed in various locations including Widcombe Crescent, and the forecourt of Widcombe Manor, overlooked by the decidedly rural church of St. Thomas-à-Becket.

Widcombe Manor is late seventeenth-century, modified in the 1720s, and in a style that might best be described as "provincial Baroque". Indeed, the design may well be by Nathaniel Ireson, who is also credited with Rosewell House in Kingsmead Square. For the visitor surfeited with Georgian grandeur (and a little pomposity too) this charming honey-coloured little mansion, set in pleasant gardens, is a real treat to the eyes. In the forecourt is a two-staged bronze fountain, late sixteenth-century, brought from a palace in Venice and nicely setting off the Venetian feel of the windows above the front porch. All this is best seen by clambering carefully round the jumble of tombstones surrounding the church for an undisturbed view at first-floor level. Just along the road is a plaque indicating that Sarah Fielding, novelist sister of Henry Fielding, lived here for many years. Like Henry she enjoyed the patronage of Ralph Allen, whose grand manor of Prior Park lies further up the hill. Entrance to the lower part of the gardens, including the farm-shop, lakes and Palladian bridge, can be obtained from Widcombe, but this is Bath, steep and demanding, and it is an excursion that is probably better completed by taking the bus to Combe Down and then walking back down through the National Trust owned gardens to Widcombe.

The main load of London-bound traffic no longer passes through **Batheaston**, a weaving village which stands where the St. Catherine's Brook enters the River Avon. Situated on a south-facing slope, it also proved an ideal place to locate market-gardens to feed hungry visitors to the city as it grew in size in the eighteenth and nineteenth centuries. Perhaps the most important feature of Batheaston is that it gives us some idea of what Bath may have looked like before 1700. There are grand old houses and cottages in vernacular styles with pretty gables and stone tile roofs, though many of them were changed to suit new fashions in the Georgian and Victorian periods. It is also a good place to celebrate the excellent work done by historical societies in places like Batheaston, Bathampton, Widcombe, Combe Down and Weston. Exhaustive research in Batheaston has pushed back the dating of many of the houses, so that buildings previously thought to be Victorian or at best Georgian can now be dated to the sixteenth and seventeenth centuries.

Like Bath itself, Batheaston very nearly became a coal community. Between 1804 and 1812 the Batheaston Mining Company sank various shafts but was unable to identify sufficient quantities of coal to make mining a commercial proposition. It was coal mania to match canal mania and (later) railway mania, but despite the involvement of the geologist and surveyor William Smith, it is doubtful whether there was ever any real prospect of finding coal. This history is quietly celebrated (with certainty) in Coalpit Lane and (possibly) The Batch (an old Somerset word for a spoil- or slag-heap). Batheaston had its own minor "Sack" in 1968, when the Lamb and Flag pub on the main road at the corner of The Batch was demolished. It had certainly existed in 1684 and at one time had been in the hands of the Fuller family. (Thomas Fuller, we have seen, was the architect of both the Newark Works of Stothert & Pitt in the Lower Bristol Road, and the Canadian Parliament building in Ottawa.) Once off the old A4 road, Batheaston becomes quieter and more obviously a village. As at Bathford and at Combe Down (where they mysteriously become "drungs"), there are a number of "drings"—pedestrian passages between high stone walls, while there are also remains of a causeway supposed to have been laid out by the monks of Bath to reach their churches at Northend (now part of Batheaston) and St. Catherine's further up this lovely valley. The word Prospect occurs and recurs: Prospect House, Prospect Buildings. A very Jane Austen word, and the view south across the water meadows to the flat top of Bathampton Down and Hill Fort is as lovely as any in the area.

At the top of Northend is Eagle House, an unlucky house if ever there was one. John Wood the Younger, architect of the Royal Crescent and Assembly Rooms, lived here, and despite his one time prosperity and fame died here in poverty in 1782. One hundred years later, at the beginning of the twentieth century, Bath had a thriving branch of the militant suffragette movement—the Women's Social and Political Union—and much of the activity was centred on Eagle House, where Mary Blathwayt and her mother Emily lived. Eagle House became a place of rest and recuperation for suffragette activists after exhausting speaking tours or the inevitable spells in prison and the horrors of forced feeding. Annie Kenney was an organizer for the WSPU in the west of England and had her own room at the house. Visiting suffragettes were encouraged to plant a tree in "Annie's Arboretum", where their photos were taken by Mary's father, Colonel Linley Blathwayt. Small metal plaques were made to commemorate each planting, and although the grounds around the house have been sold off for a small housing estate, many have survived.

Weston shares with Widcombe the distinction of being mentioned in despatches by Jane Austen as a good walk. About a mile and a half north-west of the city, it is still a pleasant walk, from Queen Square, up Gay Street, then branching off through the many pleasures of the Victoria Park, with Lansdown rising above to the right and views opening up south of the river too. There is an interesting Victorian development (Weston Park) between the park and Weston itself, comprising large detached houses that have been much in demand in recent years for hotels, private schools and care homes. The much recommended Bath Priory hotel, restaurant and spa is hereabouts, the quality of its food matched only by the quality of its gardens. A good proportion of the flowers, vegetables and fruit used in the hotel are grown in the garden under the supervision of green-fingered head gardener Jane Moore.

The village itself was once a compact collection of weavers' cottages. It has a tight little split level high street, with shops and houses on one side and the old village school and church rooms and more cottages rising above it on the north side. There is a fine pub, the King's Head, which combines a larger eighteenth-century building with a smaller house of about 1800. A great feast was held here to celebrate the passing of the 1834 Municipal Act, which brought Widcombe under the jurisdiction of the Bath Corporation, although Weston, like its twin in Twerton across the river, continued to celebrate its independence from Bath until 1951.

Slightly out of Weston, in Combe Park, is Bath's main hospital, the Royal United Hospital. Its roots lie in the city and the eighteenth century, and it is a relative newcomer to this area. Its neighbour, the Lansdown Cricket Club, may have been founded only in 1825 but has been at Combe Park since 1869. The origins of Somerset County Cricket are to be found here, rather than in distant Taunton, and W. G. Grace played at the ground on a number of occasions, as did Sir Arthur Conan Doyle. The setting may have become more crowded over the years, but with the slopes of Lansdown looming above it remains a lovely place to play the national game. Recent additions to the Combe Park scene are the St. John's Hospital Almshouses, which paradoxically sounds medieval, or at best Victorian. The St. John's

Hospital, founded in 1174 next to the hot mineral water baths and within the old city wall, was run as a business as much as a charity and over the years had accumulated considerable assets within the city. Now some of this wealth has been invested in a new twenty-first century complex that provides 54 flats, communal rooms and a chapel grouped around a central courtyard.

Combe Down, on the south side of Bath, is an interesting example of an industrial village. Until the eighteenth century it was simply the flat hilltop above the deep combe or valley in which the much older village of Monkton Combe is located. Its main use was sheep-grazing. The Romans may have quarried the Oolitic limestone known as Bath stone near here, but it was Ralph Allen who saw the possibilities of linking up with the development of Georgian Bath to make a large-scale business out of stone. He bought up land on Combe Down from the 1720s, and developed the honeycomb network of tunnels and caverns beneath the village that developed above. He also commissioned John Wood the Elder to construct a fine row of austerely classical cottages at De Montalt Place to house the quarrymen. Richard Jones, Allen's clerk of works, lived in the cottage beneath the central pediment. The quarrymen were both hard-working and hard-drinking, and several pubs had direct entrances from the underground passageways and caverns. They included the King William IV which still stands next to Ralph Allen's Yard, an abandoned workshop building at one of the entrances to the workings, 'which is now to be developed as an Interpretation Centre for the Combe Down quarry industry.

From the Combe Down quarries, a tramway carried the stone down what is now Ralph Allen Drive to Widcombe, from where it could be ferried across to the city. Later, increasing amounts of stone were shipped via the canalized Avon to Bristol and the sea. Allen built Prior Park (now a Roman Catholic private school) to showcase the qualities of Bath stone, to entertain potential customers and to offer hospitality to the writers he patronized such as Alexander Pope and Henry and Sarah Fielding. He employed Capability Brown to develop the sweeping landscape garden we see today, with its exquisite Palladian bridge. Allen's heir preferred to develop Combe Down as a health resort, but quarrying began again in the nineteenth century when much of the stone was typically carted away along the Kennett and Avon Canal to London to be used in buildings such as the west garden front of Buckingham Palace.

It was exactly such grand uses that Allen had in mind when he built Prior Park. During the nineteenth century, with the best stone exhausted, Combe Down acquired a new reputation for villa housing. The quarrymen's cottages now found a use as lodging houses for visitors, and as the homes of servants and other service workers, while the springs and fresh air enabled it to rival Weston as a laundry centre. Combe Down was also bequeathed a rather odd church, Holy Trinity. Like Beckford's tower on Lansdown it is the work of the architect Henry Goodridge. Goodridge liked Gothic and could turn his hand to formal copies of medieval precedents, as at St. Mark's in Lyncombe. But as Pevsner states, he could also be "as fanciful and crazy as the best". Go and see what you think, especially of his buttresses and pinnacles.

Twerton has played the "other" to Bath for a good many years now. Workaday, grim, dominated by factories, warehouses and the railway, Twerton is a far cry from the amenities of the city centre or the terraces and crescents of the Georgian city. It was not always so. In the Middle Ages Twerton was a wealthy village, a weaving village. It was probably from here rather than Bath itself that Chaucer's Wife of Bath would have come. In Henry Fielding's day the village straggled for the best part of a mile along the south bank of the Avon. The man who shattered Fielding's idyll in the following century was Isambard Kingdom Brunel. His Great Western Railway, having been moulded to the landscape as it crept through Sydney Gardens, exploded into assertiveness as it crossed the river and completely changed the southern end of the city as it headed westwards towards Bristol. If the crenellated ornamentation of the viaduct in the vicinity of the Churchill Bridge paid at least lip-service to Bath and to architecture, Twerton was not thought to merit such treatment. There is something stark and unflinching in the way that Brunel's Great Western Railway viaduct strides straight through the heart of Old Twerton glancing neither to left nor right. Cottages were demolished and their inhabitants offered alternative accommodation in the damp, noisy arches beneath the viaduct. Such was the power of the railway. The only redeeming feature of Brunel's Twerton was the doll's house of a railway station, closed in 1917 but so closely built into the viaduct that it has remained there ever since.

As was appropriate to a village that was everything that Bath thought itself not to be, Twerton also acquired a prison, in fact the first to be built under the 1835 Prisons Act. Only the Governor's House remains, in an unlikely Palladian style, just north of Oldfield Park station in an area usually called East Twerton. The nineteenth century was generally difficult for Twerton, with the weaving industry transforming itself from domestic to factory production in a set of "dark satanic mills" between the railway and the river. Now the mills have gone too, although the brewery has been converted into the very attractive headquarters of Somer Housing, the major social housing landlord in Bath. It is an appropriate location, since during the twentieth century, especially after the Second World War, Twerton acquired a large amount of council housing including the hastily erected and much-loved single-storey "prefabs". More substantial two-storey houses using an industrialized building system known as "Cornish Unit Housing" still survive. Twerton also became the home of Bath City Football Club, reaffirming its status as Bath's "other"—in this case the hundreds who prefer the Beautiful Game in contradistinction to the thousands who crowd to Bath rugby games. It remains there, in need of a coat of paint, but still the grand old lady of non-league football, bringing pride and distinction to a much under-rated village.

A Circle of Hills

Bath is also a city of hills, each one with its separate character and history. To the north, the Cotswold scarp of **Lansdown** rises quickly above the city to a height of some 800 feet. The dominant feature in this landscape is Beckford's Tower, with its golden cupola lovingly restored. By 1823 William Beckford was in trouble: Fonthill Abbey was crumbling; much of his inherited fortune had been dissipated. He sold Fonthill and moved reluctantly to Bath. Beckford had destroyed one of the finest Palladian mansions in England to build his Fonthill, and there was an obvious clash between his literary and artistic tastes and the dominant classical style of Georgian Bath. "Bath does not please me," he had written five years before: "After the great spectacle of the Abbey it seems to me incredibly dingy and wretched." It gets worse, with Beckford finally condemning this "paradise of idlers and corpses". Bath has come in for its fair share of criticism over the years, but this is perhaps the most cutting.

Beckford lodged in Pulteney Street and considered (rather briefly, one suspects, given his design tastes and his financial problems) buying Ralph Allen's Prior Park. Eventually he settled on Lansdown Crescent, high above the city with open countryside at his back door. He bought No. 20 and the house on the other side of a little lane, now 1 Lansdown Place West. He employed the young architect Goodridge to build a bridge at first-floor level. The bridge is still there, but Beckford soon sold the house, buying instead No. 19 to eliminate the "problem" of neighbours.

Goodridge was close to Beckford and was chosen as the architect of the tower he intended to build on Lansdown. It is impossible to fit Beckford's Tower into any style category, but Gothic it certainly is not. Perhaps "picturesque" is the closest we can come, like the elaborate landscaped garden he had built up the hillside from his home in Lansdown Crescent (unfortunately there is little of this left to see). The slim tower rises a further 150 feet above the hill, with a belvedere and lantern above it. It is not a folly; Beckford intended it more as a place to store his curiosities. Moreover, he visited it every day, to read, to move a picture here, an ornament there. Beckford was a private man, and his tower was a private retreat. It does not show itself off to the city, being visible only from the western suburbs. In the same way the view is not of the city centre, but down to Weston, across the river to Twerton, up to the skyline at Twerton Roundhill, then across to the Mendips and, on a fine day, Alfred's Tower on the Stourhead Estate. Even in a gale the tower, with its gentle internal circular staircase, has a cosy, lived-in feel about it, a good place for a self-indulgent old man who had shocked the nation in his day but now wanted to live out his days in peace. He was 66 when it was built, and 84 when he died—a life prolonged in this extraordinary building and the daily visit to it.

It is extraordinary that the National Trust turned down the tower in 1968 as of insufficient importance to merit its purchase. James Lees-Milne leapt to the defence of both Beckford and his tower, and a combination of Bath Preservation Trust, the Landmark Trust and the National Lottery have ensured that this wonderfully eccentric building lives on above the city Beckford disliked so much. Few choose to remember, however, that it was refurbished in 1833 with the money Beckford received as compensation after the abolition of slavery in the British Empire.

Lansdown's place in English history is celebrated in the discreet monument to the Battle of Lansdown, which took place during the English Civil War, away at the far north end of the down. John Wrougton's study of Civil War Bath emphasizes some of the local reasons why people inclined for the parliamentary cause. There was decline and poverty in the cloth industry, and food riots in 1630. Puritanism was a powerful force in the area, including important members of the gentry as well as tradespeople. A local pamphlet warned that the royalists were "a malignant party, who of bad guests will soon become worse masters domineering over your peace, liberties, and estates, and turning your Somersetshire into a field of blood and dead men's bones". During the brief period in 1643 when Bath was the centre of fighting, food supplies were brought in voluntarily by the people of surrounding villages.

At Lansdown Sir William Waller occupied a dominant position on the steep north slope of the hill, while Hopton and his royalist army were attacking across open land. The battle was inconclusive, with the royalists suffering more casualties but the parliamentarians retreating under cover of night into Bath. A few weeks later the royalists won decisively at Roundway Hill near Devizes and for two years Bath was under royalist control.

It is worth putting on boots to explore the battle site. This includes a very early battlefield monument, erected in 1720 by Lord Lansdown in memory of his grandfather, Sir Bevill Grenville, a Cornish royalist commander. The site is maintained by English

Heritage, and in recent years they have placed there a series of three modern marker stones, carved with designs derived from seventeenth-century publications. There are also modern interpretation panels allowing the casual visitor to get some notion of the ebb and flow of the battle. The more adventurous will take the opportunity to explore this section of the Cotswold Way along the northern scarp which was so crucial in defining the progress of the battle.

There are many pleasant ways of returning to the city on foot. It is possible to follow—at least roughly—Beckford's path back down to Lansdown Crescent, while there are numerous paths descending towards Sion Hill and Weston. Walkers can also follow the Cotswold Way down to Prospect Style and up again to Kelston Knoll, a prominent feature of this landscape. Lower than Lansdown, it is nevertheless more obviously a hill, roughly conical with the characteristic clump of trees that can be seen from as far away as Westbury White Horse in Wiltshire. From here there are fine views across the Avon valley, especially to the west and the Mendip outlier of Dundry Hill which marks the southern limits of the city and county of Bristol. From Kelston Knoll the walker can either return direct to Bath via Weston, or go down the other side of the hill to visit the pleasant hamlet of Kelston itself.

Across the other side of the city from Lansdown is **Claverton Down**, and its near neighbour Bathampton Down. Claverton Down is busy. Apart from Bath Golf Club, which occupies most of the area known as Bathampton Down, including the site of one of Bath's two prehistoric hilltop forts, the main occupants of Claverton Down are the University of Bath, the Cats and Dogs Home and the National Trust. Claverton Down is the subject of controversy in the city, but it was not always so. In the immediate post-war world of the 1950s it was a place of leisure, away from the bustle of the city centre. There was Sham Castle, the folly which Ralph Allen had caused to be built overlooking the city, to "improve" the view from his town house in Lilliput Alley. There was an area known to locals as Hampton Rocks (the remains of a number of small quarries from which stone had been shipped by a steep tramway down to Bathampton), which was a children's wonderland for scrambling, climbing, falling over and generally getting into mischief. There was Rainbow Woods, another delightful place to play with great dells which may or may not have been produced by quarrying activities at Combe Down.

The Bath Cats and Dogs Home had arrived in 1937, but was yet to achieve its present size which makes it one of the largest animal rescue centres in the country. There were playing fields close to Claverton Lane leading down to the manor and the village of Claverton in the Limpley Stoke Valley. There was by now talk of developing Claverton Down to meet the insatiable demand for housing in Bath, which had already seen much of Combe Down, Odd Down and Southdown built upon. It was at this point that the National Trust stepped in, thanks to the willingness of local landowners to sell at farmland rather than "property development" prices. The Trust purchased Rainbow Wood Farm on the southern side of the down in 1960 and the Bushey Norwood fields on its northern edge in 1960. Further fields were added in 1964. The National Trust was well on the way to securing for all time the future of Claverton Down as open space for public and agricultural use.

Enter the university—or rather the Bristol College of Science and Technology. The college was in line for upgrading to university status, and the city fathers duly stepped in and offered playing fields at Claverton to the soon-to-be university. Bristol was not amused.

It was a bold, even courageous, coup for the city. But the sudden disappearance of playing fields valued by local sports teams, and open land valued by generations of dog-walkers, picnickers and lovers, soured relationships between town and gown even before the first student moved in. Relationships have improved a little since, but it is an uneasy marriage which spills over into other bones of contention such as the impact of students lodgers on "respectable" Oldfield Park or the students' contribution to Bath's unwanted reputation as "a bit on the wild side" at weekends. It is in the nature of universities to expand, and Bath has been no different. The university has always coveted Bushey Norwood, but it is not for sale. In 1984 the National Trust secured a further 128 acres of farmland and woods stretching down almost to the city itself and including the important area of open land between Bathwick and Widcombe

Hills. The whole area was re-designated The Bath Skyline, and is superb walking country. As for the university, sometimes at sunset (and then only from a few locations in the western parts of the city) the sun will sparkle golden and red on its buildings, adding to the magic of the city. But the very effort that has gone into protecting Claverton Down means that for most people, for most of the time, the university is out of sight and out of mind.

The Cats and Dogs Home plays piggy-in-the-middle with its modest holdings between Rainbow Woods Farm and the university. Of course, dogs need exercising, and there has been excellent co-operation between the RSPCA and the National Trust to ensure that sensible use is made of both footpaths across farmland and of open access land (and that any mess is carted back to the home). Relations with the university are less good, despite the welcome efforts of student volunteers, with the university trying hard to keep dog-walkers off its land.

Away on the other side of the down, above the perilous but romantic Brassknocker Hill, is the new headquarters of Wessex Water. It is that unusual beast in Bath, a handsome new building in contemporary style, incorporating many interesting "green" features. Claverton Down, then, is a place of many wonders, but always containing potential for conflict.

The other development here in the past half-century has been the adaptation of Claverton Manor as the **American Museum in Britain**, with rooms devoted to the history, arts and crafts of the United States of America (both native American and of European settlers). There is an especially lovely collection of quilts. One of the great attractions of the museum is its setting, only just below the hilltop with open views across the exquisite Limpley Stoke Valley. Far below, the busy A36 provides a link between Bath and the south coast, but there is also the River Avon, the Kennett and Avon Canal and the railway. It is hard to imagine a more successful landscape in which human and natural activities are conjoined. Opposite, farmland rises again in the shelter of the thick Conkwell woods. The museum gardens include a replica of George Washington's flower garden at Mount Vernon, Virginia, while below is the Lewis and

Clark trail, containing trees and shrubs discovered on their pioneering expedition across the American West. A small vegetable garden, dye plant area and colonial herb garden give a flavour of how the early settlers came to terms with a very different environment.

A rocky path leads through the quarry workings on the north side of Claverton Down, green in winter and summer with moss and ferns, alive with birdsong. In winter it is muddy and slippery in wet weather, even worse in snow and ice. But through the bare skeletons of the trees can be seen the flat outline of **Solsbury Hill**, the second of Bath's prehistoric forts. It is a steady climb up from Batheaston, but rewards the visitor with spectacular views over the city and beyond. There are wildflowers in profusion on its grassy slopes and butterflies and skylarks find a happy home here. The hill was settled during the Iron Age period preceding the arrival of the Romans—about 300-100 BCE. Celtic people cleared the flat hilltop back to bare rock and built huts with timber frames and wattle walls. They must have been relatively peaceful times because only one defensive rampart was deemed necessary, built using the still familiar dry stone wall techniques, with stone on both sides and rubble infilling. Exactly why they left we shall never know, but there is archaeological evidence that the huts were burned and the rampart broken.

If Claverton Down is busy and well occupied, then the opposite is thankfully true of Little Solsbury. Just to the north, Charmy Down was the site of a Second World War airfield, used by both the RAF and USAF, closed in 1946 and decommissioned in 1949. Then in the mid-1950s, at the height of the Cold War, it was the proposed site of a radar station as part of Britain's early warning system. Preliminary work was undertaken but then abandoned. More recently there have been schemes to revive it for civilian aircraft, and it has also been used as an unofficial site by travellers. Even more recently, the local council has studied the possibility of placing a park-and-ride scheme here. Ironically, the alternative site is on the Bathampton meadows in the valley below, already the scene of one of the most vigorous of all England's anti-roads protests of the 1980s and 1990s.

Looking down from the heights of Little Solsbury into the

Avon valley beneath, there is one large blot on the landscape. This is the connecting road carved through the lower part of the hillside and onto Bathampton Meadows to make a link between the A46 road and the A4 which bypasses Batheaston. The road planners were even more ambitious, hoping to join the A46 with the A36 on the far side of the valley to create a through route from the M4 to Southampton. The confrontation between road builders and environmental campaigners reached its climax at the Whitecroft Woods, where the demonstrators, having been evicted from their camps, took to the trees, constructing tree houses, sleeping in hammocks and building elaborate walkways to connect one with another. Anthony Arlib recorded this camp and its slogans ("One world, one love"; "People need wilderness") in a series of moving black-and-white images. Such protests led directly to the passing of the 1994 Criminal Justice Act, which outlawed the work of the tree people. As Arlib put it, 1994 was a time "in which being 'green' was not a fashionable metropolitan accessory but a political choice which set you apart from the reasonable majority." The roads budget was cut but many of the plans remain in the desk drawers of planners and building contractors.

If one legacy of the roads protest is the scar of the A46/A4 link road, there are two others on Solsbury Hill. Peter Gabriel wrote and recorded a celebrated song about it, while the turf maze or labyrinth, created as a ritual protest, can still be enjoyed by those prepared to face the steep climb up the slope from Batheaston. A visitor on Good Friday 2006 also recorded on the internet an open air church service, followed by a picnic and kite flying for the children: "Everyone had walked round the different churches in Batheaston, a service at each one and carrying a wooden cross, then they had walked to the top of the hill with the cross. It was extraordinarily touching for one who doesn't believe."

III

We must stray no farther, because my task is almost at an end. It might have been possible to write about the city in its region, and wander a little more. We might have enjoyed the hamlets of the Swainswick and St. Catherine's valleys north of Bath, or the drama and the villages of the Cam and Wellow valleys south of the city. Within ten miles we might have reached Bristol, that handsome port city much loved by its inhabitants who consistently vote it one of the best places to live in England. But we cannot write of Bristol without delving into slavery on which so much of its wealth (and some of Bath's too) depends, or spending considerable time and effort on the great Brunel, his Great Western Railway, his SS *Great Britain* and his greater still Clifton Suspension Bridge. We might have included Bradford-on-Avon in Wiltshire or Frome in Somerset, sternly non-conformist weaving towns with fine seventeenth-century houses and lively cultural scenes of their own, largely independent of Bath and its festivals. But those are not tasks that I have set myself in placing on record a few thoughts on the city of Bath in which I grew up. For any author there is always another day, another book.

Further Reading

This is a list of books which I have consulted in writing my own book. I have also used a number of web-sites maintained by organisations in the city, and I would particularly like to acknowledge those belonging to religious groups, local history groups and museums. Since they can be identified by using any search-engine, it seems pointless to list them all here. For pictorial evidence, www.bathintime.co.uk is invaluable. Courtesy of the Somerset Library Service, I have also consulted some on-line reference resources, especially the Dictionary of National Biography.

Non-fiction

Aylmer, Janet, *In the Footsteps of Jane Austen through Bath to Lyncombe and Widcombe: a Walk through History*. Bath: Copperfield Books, 2003.

Beazer, Cyril, *Randon Reflections of a West Country Master Craftsman*. Privately published, 1981.

Bennet, Robert, *Selina Countess of Huntingdon: a Brief Celebration of a Remarkable Eighteenth Century Lady*. Bath: Building of Bath Collection, n/d.

Bishop, Phillippa, *Holburne Museum of Art, Bath: a Souvenir Guide*. Bath: Holburne Museum, 1999.

Borsay, Peter, *The Image of Georgian Bath 1700-2000. Towns, Heritage, and History*. London: Oxford University Press, 2000.

Brand, Horace W., *"Unwillingly to school". An Account of the Education Service in Bath*. Bath: The Education Committee of Bath City Council, 1974.

Bullamore, Tim, *Fifty Festivals: the History of the Bath Festival*. Bath: Mushroom Publishing, 1999.

Clarke, Norma, *Dr Johnson's Women*. London: Hambledon Continuum, 2001.

Cresswell, Paul (ed), *Bath in Quotes. A Literary View from Saxon Times onwards*. Bath: Crucible Publishers, 2006 (originally published by Ashgrove Press, 1985).

Crofts, Bruce (ed), *At Satan's Throne: the Story of Methodism in Bath*. Bristol: White Tree Books, 1990.

Cunliffe, Barry, *The City of Bath*. Gloucester: Alan Sutton, 1986.

Davis, Graham and Bonsall, Penny, *Bath: a New History*. Keele: Keele University Press, 1996.

Davis, Graham and Bonsall, Penny, *A History of Bath: Image and Reality*. Lancaster: Carnegie Publishing, 2006.

Dexter, Julie. *A Guide to Radstock Museum*. Radstock: Midsomer Norton and District Museum Society, 1999 (revised edition, 2002).

Drummond, Barb, *Bath Gyratory*. Privately published, 2009.

Elliott, Kirsten, *The Myth-Maker: John Wood 1704-1754*. Bath: Akeman Press, 2004.

Elliott, Kirsten and Menneer, Neil, *Bath*. London: Frances Lincoln, 2004.

Falconer, D. and Falconer, J., *Bath at War 1939-45*. Stroud: Sutton Publishing 1999.

Ferguson, Adam and Mawl, Tim, *The Sack of Bath*. Salisbury: Compton Russell, 1973.

Ferguson, Adam and Mawl, Tim, *The Sack of Bath – and after: a Record and an Indictment*. Salisbury: Michael Russell in conjunction with Bath Preservation Trust, 1989.

Forsyth, Michael (with contributions by Bird, Stephen), *Bath* (Pevsner Architectural Guides). London and New Haven: Yale University Press, 2003 (revised 2007).

Girouard, Mark, *The English Town*. London and New Haven: Yale University Press, 1990.

Goring, Edward, *By the Waters of Sul ... Bath in the Seventies* (foreword by Jan Morris). Brighton: Hermitage Books, 2006.

Haddon, John, *Portrait of Bath*. London: Robert Hale, 1982.

Jackson, Neil, *Nineteenth Century Bath Architects and Architecture*.

Bath: Ashgrove Press, 1991.

Kalinsky, Nicola, *Gainsborough*. London: Phaidon, 1995.

Lees-Milne, James, *William Beckford* (1976). London: Century, 1990.

Little, Bryan. *Bath Portrait: the Story of Bath, its Life and its Buildings*. Bristol: Burleigh Press, 1961 (second edition, 1968).

Lowndes, William, *The Theatre Royal at Bath: the Eventful Story of a Georgian Playhouse*. Bristol: Redcliffe, 1982.

Melville, Louis, *Bath under Beau Nash – and after*. London: Eveleigh Nash and Grayson, revised edition, 1926 (first published undated, but probably 1907).

Patch, Harry with van Emden, Richard, *The Last Fighting Tommy: The Life of Harry Patch, The Only Surviving Veteran of the Trenches*. London: Bloomsbury, 2008.

Payne, John, *Stothert and Pitt: the rise and fall of a Bath company*. Bath: Millstream Books, 2007.

Pevsner, Nikolaus, *The Buildings of England: North Somerset and Bristol*. Harmondsworth: Penguin Books, 1958.

Poole, Steve, 'Pitt's terror reconsidered: Jacobinism and the law in two South-Western counties, 1791-1803', *Southern History*, volume 17 (1995), pages 65-87.

Sitwell, Edith, *Bath*. London: Faber and Faber, 1932.

Sloman, Susan, *Gainsborough in Bath*. Bath: Bath and North-East Somerset Council, 1998.

Spence, Cathryn, *Bath: City on Show*. Stroud: The History Press, 2010.

Swift, Andrew, *All Roads Lead to France: Bath and the Great War*. Bath: Akeman Press, 2005.

Swift, Andrew, *The Ringing Grooves of Change: Brunel and the Coming of the Railway to Bath*. Bath: Akeman Press, 2006.

Swift, Andrew and Elliott, Kirsten, *Awash with Ale*. Bath: Akeman Press, 2004.

Swift, Andrew and Elliott, Kirsten, *The Lost Pubs of Bath*. Bath: Akeman Press, 2005.

Swift, Andrew and Elliott, Kirsten, *The Year of the Pageant*. Bath:

Akeman Press, 2009.

Todd, Janet, *Mary Wollstonecraft: a Revolutionary Life*. London: Weidenfeld and Nicolson, 2000.

Toogood, Malcolm, *Bath's Old Orchard Street Theatre*. Chippenham: Cepenpark Publishing, 2010.

Various Authors, *Pickpocketing the Rich: Portrait Painting in Bath 1720-1800*, exhibition catalogue. Bath: Holburne Museum, 2002.

Whalley, Robin, 'The Royal Victoria Park', in (ed) T. Fawcett, *Bath History*, volume 5. Bath: Millstream Books, 1994.

Wroughton, John, *A Community at War: the Civil War in Bath and North Somerset 1642-50*. Bath: The Lansdown Press, 1992.

Fiction and Poetry

Austen, Jane, *Persuasion* (1818). Oxford: Oxford University Press, 2004.

Austen, Jane, *Northanger Abbey* (1818). London: Random House, 2007.

Beckford, William, *Vathek* (1786). Oxford: Oxford University Press, 2008.

Betjeman, John, *Collected Poems*. London: John Murray, 2006.

Croft, Andy, *Time in the Shape of a Mine: Poems from Combe Down*. Bath: Bath and North-East Somerset Council, 2009.

Dickens, Charles, *Pickwick Papers* (1837). London: Oxford University Press (Oxford World's Classics), 2008.

Fielding, Henry, *Tom Jones* (1749). Oxford: Oxford University Press, 2008.

Fielding, Sarah, *The Adventures of David Simple* (1744 and 1753). Oxford: Oxford University Press, 1987.

Flint, Rose, *Mother of Pearl*. Glastonbury: PS Avalon, 2008.

Ridha, Dikra, *There are no Americans in Baghdad's Bird Market*. London: Tall Lighthouse, 2010.

Scott, Sarah, *A Description of Millennium Hall* (1762), ed Gary

Kelly. Peterborough (Ontario): Broadview Press, 1995.
Smollett, Tobias, *Humphrey Clinker* (1771), edited and introduction by Lewis M. Knapp. London: Oxford University Press, 1966.

Index